Part of the reason I find this book so compelling is that in addition to being a radical feminist and a lawyer, I have a bachelor's degree in political science, and this book is chock full of political science. But one need not be a feminist, a lawyer, or a political scientist to appreciate it. Betty McLellan's analysis and arguments are fundamentally about truth, its importance for a functioning democracy, and radical feminists' insistence on telling it. Although some of her analysis applies to her native Australia, radical feminists everywhere can learn from it. While reading, I found myself disagreeing with some of her assertions and realized that's one of the book's most essential points – in a functioning democracy, individuals and groups must be able to engage in, and tolerate, respectful dialogue and disagreement. Doing that requires a common understanding of what truth is. If we, as a global society, can get back to telling the truth (and radical feminists provide an excellent example of how to do that), maybe we can indeed save democracy.

>—Kara Dansky is an American radical feminist, lawyer, and author of the books *The Reckoning: How the Democrats and the Left Betrayed Women and Girls* and *The Abolition of Sex: How the 'Transgender' Agenda Harms Women and Girls*

Betty McLellan is a feminist ethicist and psychotherapist and the author of bestselling feminist self-help book *Help! I'm Living with a ~~Man~~ Boy,* which has been translated into 16 languages. She is also the author of *Overcoming Anxiety, Beyond Psychoppression, Ann Hannah: My (Un)Remarkable Grandmother,* and *Unspeakable: A Feminist Ethic of Speech.* With a focus on both the personal and political, Betty successfully combines her work as a psychotherapist with a broader emphasis on feminist ethical analysis and activism. She lives in Townsville, North Queensland.

Other books by Betty McLellan

Overcoming Anxiety (1992)
Beyond Psychopression: A Feminist Alternative Therapy (1995)
Help! I'm Living with a ~~Man~~ Boy (1999/2006)
Unspeakable. A Feminist Ethic of Speech (2010)
Ann Hannah: My (Un)Remarkable Grandmother (2017)

TRUTH ABANDONED

How Can Democracy Survive?

A Feminist Response

Betty McLellan

We respectfully acknowledge the wisdom of Aboriginal and Torres Strait Islander peoples and their custodianship of the lands and waterways.
The Countries on which Spinifex offices are situated are Djuru, Bunurong and Wurundjeri, Wadawurrung, Gundungarra and Noongar.

First published by Spinifex Press

Spinifex Press Pty Ltd
PO Box 200, Little River, VIC 3211, Australia
PO Box 105, Mission Beach, QLD 4852, Australia
women@spinifexpress.com.au
www.spinifexpress.com.au

Copyright © Betty McLellan, 2024

The moral right of the author has been asserted.

All rights reserved. Without limiting the rights under copyright reserved above, no part of this publication may be reproduced, stored in or introduced into a retrieval system, or transmitted, in any form or by any means (electronic, mechanical, photocopying, recording or otherwise) without prior written permission of both the copyright owner and the above publisher of the book.

Copying for educational purposes: Information in this book may be reproduced in whole or part for study or training purposes, subject to acknowledgement of the source and providing no commercial usage or sale of material occurs. Where copies of part or whole of the book are made under part VB of the *Copyright Act*, the law requires that prescribed procedures be followed. For information contact the Copyright Agency Limited.

No AI Training: Without in any way limiting the author's [and publisher's] exclusive rights under copyright, any use of this publication to 'train' generative artificial intelligence (AI) technologies to generate text is expressly prohibited. The author reserves all rights to license uses of this work for generative AI training and development of machine learning language models.

Edited by Renate Klein, Pauline Hopkins and Susan Hawthorne
Indexed by Belinda Nemec
Cover design by Deb Snibson
Typeset by Helen Christie, Blue Wren Books
Typeset in Minion
Printed and bound in Australia by Pegasus Media & Logistics

 A catalogue record for this book is available from the National Library of Australia

ISBN: 9781922964168 (paperback)
ISBN: 9781922964175 (ebook)

A cold wind of authoritarianism is blowing through our allegedly progressive, liberal-democratic society. When telling the truth becomes hate speech, when oppression becomes ethics, when non-facts become Truth, we all better look out.
—Heather Brunskell-Evans, 2018

What would happen if one woman told the truth about her life? The world would split open.
—Muriel Rukeyser (1913–1980)

Without facts, you can't have truth. Without truth, you can't have trust. Without all three, we have no shared reality and democracy as we know it – and all meaningful human endeavors – are dead.
—Maria Ressa, 2022

Contents

	Acknowledgements	xi
	Introduction	1
	Truth	3
	Democracy	5
	Feminism	10
	Liberal feminism	11
	Radical feminism	12
1.	**Feminist Focus on Truth and Truth-telling**	17
	Power	19
	Sexual exploitation	20
	Pornography	20
	Prostitution	23
	Sexual assault	25
	Surrogacy	27
	Domestic violence	28
	Discrimination on the basis of sex	32
	Language	36
	Naming	36
	Silencing	37
	Obscurantism	39
	Attempted erasure of women	41

2.	**Speaking Truth to Power**	**45**
	A note about defamation	54
3.	**Lies, Damned Lies and the Death of Democracy**	**59**
	Characteristics of a democracy	60
	Free and fair elections	60
	Power belongs to all adult citizens through their freely elected representatives	60
	Majority rules	61
	Individual rights and responsibilities	61
	Freedom of the press	61
	Independent judiciary and acceptance of the rule of law	61
	Threats to democracy	62
	Tribalism	63
	Abuse of democratic principles	64
	Ingrained inequality	69
	Political extremism	71
	Lies and disinformation	72
	How has it come to this?	78
	Neoliberalism	79
	Postmodernism	84
	Liberalism	87
	Libertarianism	88
4.	**Creative Ways of Avoiding the Truth**	**91**
	Gradualism	91
	Aged care	96
	Indigenous wellbeing	97
	Women's safety	100
	Equalism	102
	Whataboutism	108
	Waititoutism	111
	Hideandseekism	113

5. Individualism, Populism and Identity Politics — 119
    Liberalism – earlier times — 120
    Liberalism today — 121
    Liberalism's excesses — 124
        Speech — 124
        Greed — 131
            Exploitation of the less powerful — 132
            Wreaking havoc on the planet — 133
            Wanton destruction of historical sites — 134
            Sexual exploitation of women — 134
        Violence — 135
            Sexual violence — 135
            Violence in the community — 137
            Violence in relationships — 138
    Populism — 140
        Populism as a response to powerlessness — 142
        Populism as a response to contempt — 144
        Populism as a response to humiliation — 146
    Identity politics — 148

6. Leading the Way — 157
    Uncovering root causes — 159
    Changing narratives — 162
    Action across all areas — 165
    Moving forward together — 166
    A glimpse into a future that has already begun — 168
        Transgender truth and lies — 169
        Sex-based crimes against women — 170

Bibliography — 175

Index — 191

Acknowledgements

Second Wave feminism made its mark on history's pages as a movement committed to truth and truth-telling about women's situation in patriarchal society. It endeavoured to expose the untruths of the past, confront those individuals and institutions continuing to peddle lies and deceit in the present and point the way to a better future for all.

The feminist agenda, based on the belief that a common understanding of, and respect for, truth is a prerequisite for stability and harmony in any society, has always had an all-encompassing vision. While focused on the rights of women, its wider purpose is and always has been the creation of a healthier, more respectful society.

Thinking and writing here about the absolute necessity for a shared understanding of truth has focused my attention on my own personal friendship and support networks, women who share my belief that truth based on facts is an imperative.

First, I acknowledge the support of members of the Townsville Feminist Collective. In 1984, a group of us began meeting once a month for the purpose of discussing a pre-arranged set of readings on a particular topic of feminist import. Membership of the group over these 40 years has naturally waxed and waned but, always, we have been an intrepid group of truth-seekers and truth-tellers.

Here I express my gratitude for the intellectual stimulation, feminist passion and ongoing support I've shared with this group, and name current members: Meg Davis, Gail Hamilton, Nonie Harris, Ryl Harrison, Maree Hawken, Coralie McLean, Deb Miles, Chantal Oxenham, Judith Threlfall and Pauline Woodbridge.

Also, I acknowledge and name a group of feminist friends who have loved and supported me for decades, and have encouraged me to discuss my ideas as this book progressed. Originally, we were seven in number and used to call ourselves (jokingly) the Seven Sisters of Pleiades. Sadly, we've lost two of our friends in recent years (Ginni Hall and Mary Robertson) but their spirit lives on in each of us as we continue our plans to overthrow patriarchy in our lifetime! We are Coralie McLean, Gina Mercer, Bronwyn Patton, Jan Woodley – and me.

In the writing of this book, my special thanks to Coralie McLean, valued friend and confidante over many years, for her careful attention to detail as she read and re-read every page. Her commitment to feminism and her belief in radical feminist scholarship as an example of truth-telling through the ages has resulted in spirited discussions between us about the role feminism must play in saving democracy.

Finally, at this time in history when truth is often in short supply, a writer is fortunate indeed to find publishers as courageous, and as committed to truth and truth-telling, as Spinifex Press. My thanks to Renate Klein and Susan Hawthorne (publishers) and to Pauline Hopkins (editor) for their helpful comments and suggestions together with their unfailing encouragement and support.

Introduction

This is a book about feminism and democracy in which I seek to demonstrate the extent to which democracy is being threatened by today's seemingly cavalier approach to truth, and make the bold assertion that feminism itself has a pivotal role to play in saving democracy from its current slide toward oblivion.

The role feminism will play, in the future that I project, is that of shining a light on the path to a new relationship with truth and, in so doing, prepare the way for the ushering in of a renewed and reinvigorated democracy. In addition to the involvement of feminists, it is my hope that all women and men of good faith will turn their minds to how they, too, can be involved in this urgent endeavour.

First, there must be truth-telling about the past and present. There must be a confrontation with the truth about racism, misogyny, individualism, group think (sometimes called tribalism), the capture of governments by powerful business lobbies, the recalcitrance of mainstream male dominance and privilege, and the belief that lies, deceit and disinformation are legitimate forms of interacting in a whatever-it-takes-to-win environment. Second, there must be a determination to point to lies, deceit and disinformation, to speak truth to power and to demand accountability. Finally, there must be a plan to move forward and a genuine attempt to work positively with all who share the same ideals.

Every plan to move forward begins with a vision, an imagined future, and a belief that it could one day become a reality. As I prepare to articulate my own vision, I am encouraged by the thought that feminists have always imagined new futures. Who could forget Arundhati Roy's poetic words: "Another world is not only possible, she is on her way. On a quiet day, I can hear her breathing" (Roy 2003).

Or Susan Hawthorne's inspiring vision of a 'wild politics' where "diversity is central to the existence of life, to the sustenance of the planet, and to the health of human society" (Hawthorne 2002/2022, p. 369).

Or Corazon Valdez Fabros's vision of a world without war – a nuclear-free world, where peace and justice prevail. Referring to her role at the International Peace Bureau, she says, "We 'Re-imagine our World' and try our best to act for Peace and Justice" (Fabros 2021, p. 105).

Or Jess Hill's vision of a society that takes men's violence against women seriously and holds violent men accountable as a matter of urgency. Instead of the focus always being on the victim/survivor of domestic violence as in "Mary is a battered woman," Hill insists on a future where the focus is on the actions of the perpetrator, as in "John beat Mary" (Hill 2021, p. 4).

Or Maria Ressa's vision of "the world as it should be: more compassionate, more equal, more sustainable. A world that is safe from fascists and tyrants" (Ressa 2022, p. 7).

My vision, as already expressed, is that feminists will "shine a light on the path to a new relationship with truth" and, in that way, contribute to "the ushering in of a renewed and reinvigorated democracy."

This book has three major themes: truth, democracy and feminism.

Truth

Through the ages, truth and its relation to facts has been one of the central topics in philosophy. What is truth? What is the nature of truth? What, if anything, makes a truth true?

While a detailed discussion of all the philosophical theories would not be appropriate in this context, the neo-classical theory known as Correspondence Theory is the one that most closely fits with our modern-day understanding of truth. Correspondence theory, after much detailed discussion, expresses itself in a simple slogan: "A belief is true if and only if it *corresponds to a fact*" (*Stanford Encyclopedia of Philosophy* 2002, emphasis in the original).

Aristotle's well-known definition of truth bears the sentiment of that slogan:

> To say of what is that it is not, or of what is not that it is, is false, while to say of what is that it is, and of what is not that it is not, is true (in Ross 1928).

Dictionary definitions also refer to truth in terms of its relationship to facts: "The true facts about something rather than the things that have been invented or guessed" (*Oxford Dictionary*); "The real facts about a situation, event, or person" (*Cambridge Dictionary*); "The body of real things, events and facts: actuality" (*Merriam-Webster Dictionary*); "The quality of being in agreement with facts" (*Collins Australian Pocket Dictionary*).

The term 'truth-telling' is important too. As used today, it reflects a radical need for societies to pay attention to matters of justice and the need for reconciliation and healing.

South Africa's response to Apartheid in 1995 led the way. When activists finally witnessed the end of Apartheid after many decades of protests and demonstrations, they also witnessed a process designed to bring unity and reconciliation to the troubled nation. The Government of National Unity under President

Nelson Mandela established the Truth and Reconciliation Commission (1995) whose purpose was to uncover the truth about human rights' violations by hearing from both victims and perpetrators, but not prosecuting people for past crimes. It was the act of truth-telling that was to bring healing to the nation. Archbishop Desmond Tutu was appointed Chair of the Commission. The hearings were open and transparent and, while the Commission confronted many challenges and limitations, South Africa's Truth and Reconciliation Commission is regarded internationally as successful.[1]

Truth-telling is a term also used by Indigenous Australians. Ever since colonisation, when the British invaders proclaimed that Australia was *terra nullius* (empty land), Indigenous Australians have suffered oppression, theft of their children and land, violence and death at the hands of non-Indigenous people and institutions. In 2017, a group of Indigenous Australians produced the *Uluru Statement from the Heart*, aimed at healing, reconciliation and "a fair and truthful relationship" with the rest of Australia. The statement recognised, however, that such a relationship would only be possible after a process of "truth-telling about our history."[2]

While the statement was rejected, seemingly without consideration, by the government led by Prime Minister Malcolm Turnbull in 2017 and ignored by the subsequent government of Prime Minister Scott Morrison, Indigenous leaders, nevertheless, kept it alive as an offer of peace and reconciliation on the understanding that truth-telling is still central. The Labor government of Prime Minister Anthony Albanese, elected to office on 21 May 2022, promised to prepare the way for a nation-wide referendum on including a First Nations Voice

---

1 <https://www.justice.gov.za/trc>.
2 <https://ulurustatement.org>.

in the Constitution. Once the voice had the protection of the Constitution, it was believed, truth-telling would go ahead on equal terms. The Minister for Indigenous Affairs, Linda Burney, agreed that truth-telling must be front and centre of all future negotiations.

The Referendum held on 14 October 2023 asked the Australian people to vote on a very simple proposal:

> ... to alter the Constitution to recognise the First Peoples of Australia by establishing an Aboriginal and Torres Strait Islander Voice.

The proposal was rejected by a large margin – 40% Yes, 60% No. It remains to be seen what progress, if any, will be made on the other parts of the Uluru Statement, which called for Voice, Treaty, Truth.[3]

The fight for women's rights, too, begins with truth-telling. As already mentioned, speaking truth to power requires courage and an ability to persist in the face of resistance, denial and possible punishment for the truth-teller. Fortunately, feminist researchers, writers and activists have courage in abundance as the brief review of Second Wave feminist literature in Chapter One will reveal.

Democracy

Defining democracy is not an easy task, given that there are many different types of democracy throughout the world. In fact, according to Jean-Paul Gagnon, social and political philosopher at the University of Canberra, as many as 2,234 adjectives have been used to describe democracy (Gagnon 2018).

Most attempts at defining democracy begin by explaining that the word 'democracy' comes from the Greek words 'demos'

---

[3] For more discussion on the Referendum loss, see Chapter Four.

(people) and 'kratos' (rule) – rule by the people. If it is to function properly, says Robert Longley in a piece attempting to define democracy, it is "a system of government that not only allows but requires the participation of the people in the political process" (Longley 2021).

Democracy is often defined by its ideals and principles. As set out by Australia's Parliamentary Education Office, the ideals of democracy include:

- Active and engaged citizens
- Respect for individuals
- Freedom of speech and association
- An inclusive and equitable society
- Free and franchised elections
- The rule of law for both citizens and government.[4]

The above ideals are reflected in the general principles of democracy, which include: majority rule (governments are elected by majority vote of the people); free and fair elections; separation of powers; equality before the law; human rights; freedom of speech, religion and assembly; property rights; freedom of the press; and freedom from unwarranted government interference.[5]

In addition to ideals and principles, democracy is also explained by reference to the different types of democracy in play around the world:

Direct democracy is a system in which citizens have the right to present their views directly to the government. In Switzerland, for example, all citizens receive information brochures on issues to be decided by the government on all levels (country, Kanton

---

4 <https://peo.gov.au/understand-our-parliament/how-parliament-works/system-of-government/democracy/>.
5 <https://www.aph.gov.au/About_Parliament/House_of_Representatives/About_the_House_News/News/Parliament_Explained_Democracy>.

and Council) and have the option of sending their ballot papers back to the government by post.

Representative democracy is a system in which the political power of the people is exercised through elected representatives who are tasked with the responsibility of listening to the views of the people in their electorates and then representing those views to government. The United States, the United Kingdom, France, Germany and Australia are a few examples of countries where representative democracy is strong.

Parliamentary democracy is a representative democracy with a House of Representatives and, in most cases, an upper house (House of Lords in the United Kingdom, and the Senate in Australia). The United Kingdom has a constitutional monarch with limited powers and Australia has a Governor-General also with limited powers.

Presidential democracy, or Republicanism, is also a representative democracy with governments being elected to office by the citizens. A significant difference between presidential and parliamentary democracies is that a President is directly elected by the people while a Prime Minister is elected by his or her own political party. The leader of the party that wins an election automatically becomes Prime Minister.

Constitutional democracy is a representative democracy that limits the power of the Government via a set of rules, a Constitution, which cannot be changed except by vote of the majority of citizens. The United States is a presidential-constitutional democracy, and Australia is a parliamentary-constitutional democracy.

Liberal democracy, too, is a representative democracy and is a term often used to emphasise the rights and freedoms of individual citizens. In the context of this book, the category 'liberal democracy' requires a slightly more extensive description than the others, so I include the following.

Sometimes the terms 'liberal' and 'democracy' are used interchangeably as if they are the same but, while they share some similarities, there are distinct differences that cannot be ignored. In particular, liberalism is a political philosophy, a belief system that emphasises individual rights and freedoms; whereas democracy is a system of government in which power is vested in the people and maximum participation is encouraged. Liberalism calls for government intervention to promote equality of opportunity, to address problems caused by inequality and to provide support through affordable healthcare and well-funded welfare programs.[6]

Liberalism is not influenced by democracy but democracy can be, and most often is, influenced by liberalism. It is important, therefore, to mention liberalism's early history before moving on.

While the Magna Carta, signed by King John of England in 1215, marked a turning point in the quest for recognition of human rights for free men, it is generally held that liberalism had its beginnings in the Age of Enlightenment (seventeenth and eighteenth centuries) with philosopher John Locke (1632–1704) often referred to as 'the father of liberalism'. Other Enlightenment thinkers advocating individual freedoms and the use of reason to seek the truth include Thomas Hobbes (1588–1679), Jean-Jacques Rousseau (1712–1778), and Immanuel Kant (1724–1804). Proponents of liberalism sought to replace conservatism, the divine right of Kings, hereditary privilege, state religion and so on, with a focus on individual rights, individual freedoms, secularism and democracy.

---

6   In contrast, libertarianism prioritises individual liberty, promotes personal choice and insists on limited government intervention in the lives of citizens. The belief that the pursuit of one's own happiness is the true purpose of life places libertarianism in opposition to democratic values.

INTRODUCTION

An important advocate for liberalism in the nineteenth century was John Stuart Mill (1806–1873). His *On Liberty* (1859) has been called "one of the most celebrated defences of free speech ever written"[7] although, as Helen Pringle points out, Mill never actually used the phrase 'freedom of speech' in *On Liberty*. What he defends is liberty, "the sovereignty of the individual" (Pringle 2022). In addition to his arguments for freedom of the individual, he defends what later became known as the harm principle. While asserting that individuals have absolute sovereignty over themselves and ought to be free to develop their own characters, he makes one exception: "The only purpose for which power can be rightfully exercised over any member of a civilised community, against his will, is to prevent harm to others" (Mill 1999, p. 73).

Mill also wrote *The Subjection of Women* in which he argued for complete equality between the sexes. In his autobiography, he describes his relationship with his wife, Harriet Taylor Mill, as "a partnership of thought, feeling and writing." He states that, for the two years before his retirement from official life, they were "working together on *Liberty*." He continues:

> After it had been written as usual twice over, we kept it by us, bringing it out from time to time and going through it anew, reading, weighing, and criticising every sentence (Mill 1873, p. 156).

Devastated by Harriet's untimely death, he reflected on how much richer his writing was because of his wife's influence. They both were committed to democracy but, he added, Harriet was also a socialist and that challenged him to expand his concept of liberty to include the need for societies to lift the poor out of poverty in order that they, too, would be in a position to aim for

---

7   <https://www.libertarianism.org/columns/introduction-john-stuart-mills-liberty>.

liberty. To summarise, liberalism, according to John Stuart Mill and Harriet Taylor Mill, involved sovereignty of the individual, care that the exercise of one's own sovereignty did not impinge on the sovereignty of others, equality between the sexes and lifting the poor out of poverty so that liberty would be available to all.

While there are many types of democracy in play, Kofi Annan, former Secretary-General of the United Nations, focuses attention on some of the important features that tie them all together. In a speech at the Athens Democracy Forum in 2017, titled 'The Crisis of Democracy', he said:

> I have been a tireless defender of democracy all my life because I am convinced it is the political system most conducive to peace, sustainable development, the rule of law and the respect for human life … (Annan 2017).

Feminism

Contrary to the popular belief that has circulated in recent years, feminism is not simply a lifestyle choice or an identity a woman picks up when she wants to appear sassy or empowered. Feminism is, as it has always been, a political movement aimed at exposing the structural inequalities that exist in society, speaking out against the built-in misogyny that still influences government policies and decision-making, and holding individual men to account for their attitudes and behaviour toward women.

In 1978, Alison Jaggar and Paula Rothenberg Struhl wrote about the different types of feminism they identified as being in place at that time: Conservatism, Liberalism, Traditional Marxism, Radical Feminism and Socialist Feminism. Their book, *Feminist Frameworks*, discusses in important detail the differences in approach taken by feminists in their attempts to unravel the mysteries surrounding relationships between women and men (Jaggar and Struhl 1978, pp. 67–155).

While the Marxist and Socialist strands of feminism have taken a back seat today, Liberal and Radical feminism are as prominent as they ever were.[8]

Liberal feminism

The politics of liberal feminism have changed significantly over the years and, while I am highly critical of today's version, I cannot forget the positive role many liberal feminists played in the decades before the turn of the millennium. While radical feminists were always the vanguard of the movement, agitating from the margins, protesting, demonstrating against the systems that were keeping women powerless, liberal feminists were willing to work within the patriarchal system with the aim of bringing about change from within. They were criticised by some, and labelled 'femocrats' in Australia, but the reality is that they fought hard and achieved many significant changes such as legislation against sexual harassment, against rape in marriage and against men's violence in relationships. Also, as radical feminists put pressure on governments from external vantage points to fund women's refuges, domestic violence services, rape crisis services and women's centres in general, liberal feminists applied pressure from within the government departments where they worked. The task of liberal feminists was a difficult one and the role they played in easing the burden for women should not be forgotten.

Apart from that, the story is not so positive. The liberal emphasis on 'choice' and 'freedom' saw liberal feminists support-

---

[8] Since the 1990s, new 'types' of feminism have emerged, including postmodern feminism, queer feminism, intersectional feminism and so-called trans feminism. It is not my intention, however, to elaborate on these types here.

ing prostitution, pornography and surrogacy regardless of the harm those industries wreaked on women. Still today, they maintain that it is an individual woman's right to 'choose' to be involved in such practices, whereas radical feminists maintain that such industries are exploitative, violent and dangerous, and continue to call for their abolition. Sadly today, many liberal feminists, influenced by identity politics, offer their support indiscriminately in the name of (arguably, a wrong interpretation of) intersectionality,[9] including supporting the demands of transgender activists to the detriment of biological women.

Radical feminism

Radical feminism is feminism uncompromised and uncompromising when it comes to fighting for the rights of women. Because of their unwillingness to compromise their values, radical feminists are sometimes labelled essentialist or conservative, also stubborn, unbending and single-minded. Indeed, the term radical feminism has such a bad reputation that trans activists use it as a put-down against anyone who expresses the slightest disagreement with them and their agenda. Even those who claim no affiliation with feminism at all can be called 'trans exclusionary radical feminists' (TERFs) when they dare to disagree.

But radical feminists, mindful of the seriousness of their political agenda, will not be deterred by the bad reputation. Women are suffering from entrenched exploitation and violence against them, and the radical view is that the seriousness of women's predicament calls for truth, not compromise. Men's violence against women is wrong, as is the sex industry's exploitation of women and the trans industry's attempt to erase women. It is not compromise that is needed, say radical feminists, it is

---

[9] For more on intersectionality, see Chapter Five.

INTRODUCTION

change – change in men's attitudes and behaviour, and change in the structures of society that still favour men at every turn.

Robin Morgan described the role of radical feminism very powerfully:

> What radical feminists have in common ... includes a stubborn commitment to the people of women, the courage to dare question anything and dare redefine everything, a dedication to making connections between issues, a sobering comprehension of the enormity of this task – freeing more than half of humanity and, by so doing, saving the other half ... (Morgan 1996, p. 7).

Feminism in its radical form dares to question everything as it appears on the surface, analyses situations at depth, shines a light on the root causes of women's oppression, and demands change.

◇◇◇

In Chapters One and Two, I begin by pointing to the truths told by feminists. The review of Second Wave feminist literature in Chapter One, while certainly not an exhaustive historical account, nevertheless reveals feminism's disenchantment with liberal democracy and makes the point that the radical feminist endeavour has always been about speaking truth to power. Then, in Chapter Two, I present examples of truth-telling today, once again revealing the courage of feminists and other women determined to expose the truth about their experiences of sexual abuse, harassment, violence, rape and other humiliations at the hands of men and of male-focused institutions.

From there, I turn my attention, in Chapters Three, Four and Five, to the alarming circumstances undermining democracy today: deliberate lies and disinformation, 'creative' language meant to deceive, and a focus on the corrosive effects of individualism.

In Chapter Three, I express concern at the fact that lies are becoming so commonplace as to be expected and, by some, even accepted. Here, I delve into some of the concerns feminists and other social justice activists have about the disdain recent leaders (in particular, the USA's President Donald Trump, the UK's Prime Minister Boris Johnson and Australia's Prime Minister Scott Morrison) had for democracy itself. The record of lies told by each of those leaders speaks for itself and causes alarm about the damage done to democracy.

In Chapter Four, I continue in my exploration of truth with a focus on the many politicians and other leaders whose aim it is to hold on to power and control at any cost, and I point to the 'creative' ways they have developed for the purpose of avoiding the truth. Sometimes their methods are so well camouflaged that citizens are lulled into thinking that the issues they are concerned about are actually being dealt with by those in authority when they are not. Here I shine a light on some of the undemocratic methods used by those in power in an attempt to deceive.

Still focusing on those circumstances undermining democracy, I turn my attention, in Chapter Five, to today's obsession with individualism, personal freedoms and identity politics, and explore the social and psychological damage resulting from such an obsession.

Finally, in Chapter Six, believing that a universal commitment to truth is essential if democracy is to be saved from its current slide toward oblivion, I set out elements of a radical feminist plan to lead the way. With that, I implore politicians, business leaders and citizens alike to find the courage to follow the example of radical feminists, whistleblowers and others who value their integrity above all else, and commit themselves to truth regardless of the consequences.

While the focus on lies, disinformation, deceit and trickery of language throughout the book may appear to be somewhat dark, the final chapter is full of light and optimism about the future. Feminists and others who refuse to be compromised are invited to glimpse a future where truth prevails – and celebrate.

CHAPTER ONE

Feminist Focus on Truth and Truth-telling

Second Wave feminism, from its beginnings in the 1960s and 1970s, was a demand for the truth to be told about women's oppression by men and male institutions.

Previous uprisings of women had made similar demands. The US Seneca Falls Convention in 1848, organised by Elizabeth Cady Stanton, Lucretia Mott and others, concluded with the release of the Declaration of Sentiments that began:

> We hold these truths to be self-evident; that all men and women are created equal. The history of mankind is a history of repeated injuries and usurpations on the part of man toward woman, having in direct object the establishment of an absolute tyranny over her. To prove this, let the facts be submitted to a candid world.[10]

There followed 16 facts intended to shine a light on the truth of women's oppression. The Declaration was signed by 68 women present at the Convention and 32 men who registered their support for the movement by attending the Convention.[11]

---

10 National Park Service. n.d. 'Declaration of Sentiments'. <https://www.nps.gov/wori/learn/historyculture/declaration-of-sentiments.htm>.
11 Following in the footsteps of the brave women at the Seneca Falls Convention, feminists today have made a new Declaration: The Women's Declaration International (WDI), the aims of which are outlined in Chapter Six.

In the early years of the twentieth century, the Suffragette movement in the UK focused on women's right to vote. There were actually two groups: the Suffragists led by Millicent Garrett Fawcett, and the Suffragettes led by Emmeline Pankhurst. While the groups used different tactics, their aim of achieving women's right to vote was the same. They were determined to draw attention to the fact that men's refusal to allow women equal access to voting on the grounds that they were emotional beings and, therefore, unable to understand and analyse hard political matters, was a lie. The real reason for excluding women was to ensure that power stayed in the hands of men. While the movement for women's suffrage began as a single-issue movement led by middle class women, it expanded to include a focus on labour conditions and the poverty working class women struggled with.

The next uprising of women, now known as Second Wave feminism, had a broad-ranging focus on patriarchal dominance. Incorporating the demands of previous uprisings and having a special emphasis on men's violence against women, facts were laid out and demands made. Feminists, through their writing and activism, made it clear that they were no longer willing to settle for lies or superficial 'explanations' about the second-class status of women. Using women's everyday experiences as empirical evidence, they revealed these truths: women were discriminated against from birth; women were victims of men's violence in all its forms; women were commodified and used for the benefit of men; women were blamed when men raped and abused them; and women were held responsible for their husbands' and children's problems. It became clear through comprehensive and painstaking feminist analysis, that women were either excluded and ignored, or sexualised and trivialised.

Determined to reveal the truth, Second Wave feminists wrote about many issues, including power, sexual exploitation, domestic violence, discrimination, language and patriarchy's attempted erasure of women.

Power

Hannah Arendt's essay 'Truth and Politics' published in *The New Yorker* on 25 February 1967, is an early example of the unmasking of patriarchal power by Second Wave feminists. It may seem strange that I am including Arendt's work here seeing as she was, in fact, opposed to the Women's Liberation Movement on the grounds that women would lose more than they would gain. She preferred to be seen as 'feminine' rather than 'feminist'. Nevertheless, Hannah Arendt and her fearless writing have been lauded by feminists since the 1970s. To this day, she remains a hero of the feminist movement for her steadfastness and courage in confronting the male establishment. She was ruthless, for example, in her evaluation of how politicians handled the truth. Her essay on 'Truth and Politics' begins with the words: "No one has ever doubted that truth and politics are on rather bad terms with each other."

Arendt's essay was written in response to the controversy that followed the publication of her book *Eichmann in Jerusalem*. She was attacked by politicians and others for presenting Eichmann as "a dull official who was just doing his job." They wanted him portrayed as "evil and demonic" but Arendt, who attended every day of his trial, saw him as "an unimaginative bureaucrat who was simply obeying orders" (Heberlein 2020, pp. 190–191). The attacks by politicians were fierce and personal. "What most worried her," wrote Samantha Rose Hill of the Hannah Arendt Center for Politics and the Humanities, "was a form of political propaganda that uses lies to erode reality. Political power, she warned, will always sacrifice factual truth for political gain" (Hill 2020).

Arendt compares rational truth and factual truth. Rational truth can change its nature and become opinion and interpretation, but factual truth is different:

> Facts are beyond agreement and consent, and all talk about them ... will contribute nothing to their establishment. Unwelcome opinion can be argued with, rejected, or compromised upon, but unwelcome facts possess an infuriating stubbornness that nothing can move except plain lies (Arendt 1967).

While Hannah Arendt highlighted the relationship between truth and politics in this essay, much of Second Wave feminist writing from the 1970s up to today has focused attention on the misuse of power by men and male-dominated institutions in a variety of areas. As illustrated throughout this chapter, feminists exposed the fact that truth is sacrificed in pursuit of power, privilege and financial gain through sexual exploitation in its many forms (pornography, prostitution, sexual assault, surrogacy) and through men's violence against women in the home.

Sexual exploitation
Pornography

While proponents have always presented pornography as harmless and insisted that the production and use of pornography is a free speech issue, staunch radical feminist Kathleen Barry named it the propaganda of woman hatred (Barry 1979). Andrea Dworkin's *Pornography: Men Possessing Women*, first published in 1979, states clearly and unapologetically that pornography is about men's power over women. The opening paragraph of the book's preface reads:

CHAPTER ONE: FEMINIST FOCUS ON TRUTH AND TRUTH-TELLING

> This is a book about the meaning of pornography and the system of power in which pornography exists. Its particular theme is the power of men in pornography (Dworkin 1979).

The word 'pornography' comes from the ancient Greek and means 'writing about whores', she explains, "specifically and exclusively the lowest class of whore … She was simply and clearly and absolutely, a sexual slave" (Dworkin 1979, pp. 199–200).

In response to the widely held belief that pornography merely represents 'depictions of the erotic', that the sex isn't real because the women are actors, Dworkin draws attention to the fact that modern technology presents real women being debased for the pleasure of men:

> Real women are tied up, stretched, hanged, fucked, gang-banged, whipped, beaten, and begging for more … To profit, the pimps must supply (what the market is demanding) … women being brutalised and loving it (1979, pp. 201–202).

Catharine MacKinnon, speaking at the Ninth Annual Commonwealth Law Conference in Auckland, New Zealand, in 1990, reminded participants that "women and children are every moment being violated to make pornography, brutalized through its consumption, bought and sold in this technologically sophisticated slave traffic" (in MacKinnon 2006, p. 112).

Drawing attention to the brutality, the hatred of women and the racial hatred evident in pornography, MacKinnon said:

> Women in pornography are bound, battered, tortured, harassed, raped, and sometimes killed … Asian women are presented so passive they cannot be said to be alive, bound so that they are not recognizably human, hanging from trees and light fixtures and clothes hooks in closets. Black women are presented as animalistic bitches, bruised and bleeding, struggling against their bonds. Jewish women orgasm in reenactments of death camp tortures (2006, pp. 114–115).

In 1983, Dworkin and MacKinnon presented a Feminist Ordinance against Pornography[12] to the City of Minneapolis. This Ordinance, described as "a sex equality law, a civil rights law, a law that says that sexual subordination through pictures and words, this sexual traffic in women, violates women's civil rights" (MacKinnon 1990, p. 9), was passed by the Minneapolis City Council on 30 December 1983. However, it never actually became law in Minneapolis because it was vetoed by the mayor, reintroduced in 1984, passed again and vetoed again.

In vetoing the Ordinance, Dworkin said, the mayor

> ... claimed that it would violate the constitutional rights of the pornographers, which superseded in importance the speech rights of women and children who were shut up by pornography" (Dworkin 2004, p. 137).

Since that time, feminist writing has continued to emphasise the harm pornography does to all women, not just the women who are paid to participate in the filming, nor the women whose male partners insist on acting out with them the degrading and violent sex they view on their computers, but all women (Russell 1993; MacKinnon 1994; MacKinnon and Dworkin 1997). Pornography legitimates domination and subordination (Gaze 1994). It subordinates women (Itzin 1992). Not only does it depict and cause subordination, but it is, "in and of itself, a form of subordination" (Langton 1994). It silences women (MacKinnon 1994; Langton 1994; McLellan 2010). It is hate propaganda (Barry 1979; Stark and Whisnant 2004). It is an industry, making huge profits off the subordination, silencing, violence and woman-hating that pornography represents (Stark and Whisnant 2004; Jeffreys 2009; Dines 2010; Tankard Reist and Bray 2011).

---

12 For details of the public hearings, see Catharine MacKinnon and Andrea Dworkin (Eds), 1997, *In Harms Way: The Pornography Civil Rights Hearings.*

Prostitution

While so-called 'progressives' in democratic countries name prostitution as sex work and promote it as 'a job like any other', and while liberal and libertarian feminists speak of 'sex work' as a legitimate choice for women, radical feminists have worked hard at uncovering the truth of prostitution. Prostitution, like trafficking, is described in terms of the buying and selling of women, where the power is in the hands of the buyer. Women and their sexual services are bought and are, therefore, subject to the buyers' demands.

Melissa Farley, a researcher and clinical psychologist, founded Prostitution Research and Education in San Francisco in 1995. A non-profit organisation conducting research on prostitution, pornography and trafficking, its goal is nothing less than abolishing prostitution and the "assumption that men are entitled to buy women for sex." The organisation makes its research available to all who request it, and consults with agencies working with women escaping prostitution.[13] Farley, who has immersed herself in this area of research and activism for many years, says:

> There is a selfish reason why we non-prostituted women need to understand the experience of women in prostitution: because our worst nightmares are their daily experiences, and because they understand so clearly what misogyny in action feels and looks like (Farley 2018a).

There are huge risks involved for women who are "consumed as a commodity" in prostitution, writes Farley:

> For most of the world's prostituted women, prostitution is the experience of being hunted, dominated, harassed, assaulted and battered. Despite the fact that money is paid, sexual assault

---

[13] <prostitutionresearch.com>.

remains most women's experience of prostitution (Farley 2018b, pp. 97–108).

Women around the world enter prostitution for a number of reasons, she writes, including poverty, homelessness and unemployment. Studies show that many prostituted women are victims/survivors of childhood sexual abuse who enter prostitution because they see themselves as 'good for nothing but sex'. Others see it as a way of being paid for the abuse they used to endure for free (Farley 2003, pp. 247–280). Andrea Dworkin called incest a 'boot camp' for prostitution (Dworkin 1997, pp. 139–151).

The harms of prostitution are many. Those survivors who escape the sex industry attest to the fact that the lifestyle causes harm to the mental health of women caught up in it: depression, self-loathing, dissociation, PTSD, alcohol/drug dependence, eating disorders and others. Harms to their physical health and safety include: sexually transmitted infections, HIV/AIDS, uterine infections, menstrual problems, ovarian pain, infertility, pregnancy, violence, sexual abuse and rape (Farley 2003; Jeffreys 2004; Sullivan 2004; Bindel 2017).

Sheila Jeffreys' work, *The Idea of Prostitution* (1997), was aimed at "transforming the way that prostitution is thought about" (p. 5). She concludes her comprehensive analysis by suggesting that the truth of prostitution be taken seriously. Instead of accepting the idea that prostitution is "natural, inevitable, and justified," she appeals to those concerned about women's human rights to acknowledge "that prostitution is a form of brutal cruelty on the part of men that constitutes a violation of women's human rights, wherever and however it takes place" (Jeffreys 1997, p. 348).

Prostitution as a violation of women's human rights is central to the work of The Coalition Against Trafficking in Women

(CATW). CATW is an international organisation "working to end the trafficking and sexual exploitation of women and girls."[14] Established in 1988, its first director was Kathleen Barry whose work in this area is widely respected, followed later by other such prominent feminists as Dorchen Leidholdt and Janice G. Raymond. Currently, the Executive Director is Taina Bien-Aimé and the President of the Board of Directors is long-time CATW member and activist, Aurora Javate-De Dios from the Philippines.

Echoing the words of United Nations Secretary General, António Guterres who declared: "Every woman and every girl has the right to a life free from violence," CATW stated:

> Living free from violence and discrimination is a fundamental human right. It is a necessity to achieving sustainable peace and development around the world. Yet, women and girls face violence and discrimination every day *because* they are women and girls.[15]

Prostitution (the trafficking of women for sex) as a violation of women's human rights has continued as the main theme in radical feminist writing on the issue (Leidholdt 1993; MacKinnon 1993; Barry 1995, 2012; Dworkin 1997; Stark and Whisnant 2004; Sullivan 2007; Raymond 2013, 2015; Norma and Tankard Reist 2016; Hunter 2022; Smiley 2023).

Sexual assault

When my grandfather repeatedly raped his step-daughter (my aunt) from age seven into her mid-teens, from approximately 1910 to 1920, the sexual abuse of children by their fathers was virtually ignored because men were free to do as they pleased with their own families, and there were no support services

---

14   <catwinternational.org>.
15   ibid.

where daughters and their mothers could go for help (McLellan 2017). Sigmund Freud refused to believe that such monstrous things happened, preferring to believe that the truth revealed to him by many of his women patients was simply fantasy on their part (Masson 1989).

When Second Wave feminists began speaking and writing about their own and other women's childhood experiences of sexual abuse, it opened up the floodgates and allowed the truth to come out (Armstrong 1978, 1994; Rush 1980; Herman 1981; Jeffreys 1982; Ward 1984; Easteal 1994). They also wrote about rape and other forms of sexual assault that teenagers and adult women were subjected to both inside and outside the home (Millett 1972; Brownmiller 1975; Russell 1975, 1990; Kelly 1989; Herman 1994; MacKinnon 1994; Hattingh 2017).

To this day, the numbers of women revealing that they have been raped by men on dates, men of their acquaintance, fellow students and work colleagues is astounding. The truth is being told, but with patriarchal law enforcement agencies still set up to favour perpetrators, statistics show that justice is rarely achieved for victims/survivors. In their book *How Many More Women?* lawyers Jennifer Robinson and Keina Yoshida expose the many ways that the law silences women who speak out about sexual abuse:

> The spike in survivors speaking out has been followed by a spike in legal actions against them and the journalists who want to report their stories – in defamation, in contract, in privacy and in breach of confidence ... The law is being wielded to reinforce the culture of silence and protect the status quo (Robinson and Yoshida 2022, p. 4).

Surrogacy

In 1984, feminists from various countries came together to discuss their concerns about reproductive and genetic engineering and the harmful effects of those practices on women. As a result, the Feminist International Network on the New Reproductive Technologies (FINNRET) was formed. The following year, an important conference was held in Bonn, Germany, at which, writes Renate Klein, "(m)ore than 2000 participants issued a clear *No* to the technological take-over of women's reproduction and lives" (Klein 2017, p. 108). Soon after, at an 'Emergency Conference' in Sweden, a decision was made to change the name of the Network from FINNRET to FINRRAGE (Feminist International Network of Resistance to Reproductive and Genetic Engineering). So, the powerful network FINRRAGE was born in 1985.[16] Members were determined to reveal the truth about reproductive technologies, genetic engineering and surrogacy. They wanted to expose the power dynamics at play, with the rampant takeover of women's natural reproductive capacity by the medical professions and medical technologies.

Many books and articles were published (Arditti, Klein and Minden (Eds) 1984/1989; Corea 1985; Mies 1985; Spallone and Steinberg (Eds) 1987; Scutt (Ed.) 1988/1989; Akhter, Van Berkel and Ahmed (Eds) 1989; Klein 1989b; Klein 1989c; Akhter 1992; Rowland 1992; Raymond 1993/1994).

In 1989, FINRRAGE held a conference in Comilla, Bangladesh, in conjunction with the Bangladeshi organisation UBINIG (Policy Research for Development Alternative). Participants produced a powerful piece of work called the Comilla Declaration (Akhter, Van Berkel and Ahmed 1989). In her paper to the conference, Farida Akhter explained:

---

16 <http://www.finrrage.org>.

> At FINRRAGE, we ... resist technologies ... that are being produced at this phase in history where patriarchal relations are the dominant mode of relation of reproduction. By resisting patriarchal technologies, we are actually resisting patriarchy (Akhter 1989, pp. 8–11).

Renate Klein, in her paper to the conference pointed to the "increased control over women's fertility":

> I wish to emphasize that all forms of biomedical intervention from surrogate motherhood to genetic screening and sex selection must be seen on a continuum and as intrinsically linked with one another: they share the ideology that human reproduction should be taken out of women's hands and instead be controlled by doctors, scientists and, increasingly the state.

When there are 'chosen' babies, 'made to order', she asks: "who profits?" and "who pays the price?" (Klein 1989a, pp. 12–18).

As the baby-buying industry flourished around the world, typically wealthy couples from western nations commissioning women from poorer countries to be their 'gestational carriers', feminists continued to voice their strong objections. Jennifer Lahl called for truth-telling in her 2016 article, 'Telling the Truth about Surrogacy in the United States' (Lahl 2016/2022), while Renate Klein called it "a human rights violation" in her 2017 book *Surrogacy: A Human Rights Violation* (Klein 2017).

Heartbreaking stories from surrogate mothers can be found also in Jennifer Lahl, Melinda Tankard Reist and Renate Klein (Eds), *Broken Bonds: Surrogate Mothers Speak Out* (2019).

Domestic violence

When women began meeting together in small groups in each other's homes in the 1960s and early 1970s, the ugly truth about the extent and severity of men's violence against women in the home began to surface. These meetings came to be known as consciousness-raising groups and were the catalyst for the huge uprising of women around the world. As the truth came out and women realised that the violence they had been experiencing privately was, in fact, a common experience of women everywhere, the Women's Liberation Movement began.

Radical feminists, determined to "break the silence about domestic violence,"[17] encouraged women to speak out about their own experiences of violence in the home. When Germaine Greer wrote: "Women have very little idea of how much men hate them," she went on to illustrate the loathing and disgust boys learn to feel toward girls from a young age (Greer 1971, p. 249).

Erin Pizzey wrote her ground-breaking book *Scream Quietly or the Neighbours will Hear* in 1974. Being made aware of the isolation and loneliness many women in the UK were feeling, Pizzey and a few friends decided to form 'Women's Aid' and to look for a place where women could meet and talk. The Borough of Hounslow gave them the keys to a derelict house that they were able to work on with a little help from others, and it wasn't long before it was transformed into a comfortable base for Women's Aid. Following media interviews, women began writing to Women's Aid while others just dropped in to the house, often with their children, wanting to talk about the extreme violence they had endured from their husbands for many years. Pizzey's book is full of heart-breaking stories. A letter from a woman in Brighton begins:

> Please could you advise me what to do ... My husband keeps saying I'm mad and keeps hitting and whipping me. I've had a broom over my head and needed medical treatment, a

---

[17] This was a popular chant at protest rallies and marches in the 1970s and 1980s.

dislocated shoulder, bruises all over me and two black eyes and kicked in the ribs ...

He has thrown me out at night and told me to go but I can't leave the children ... (Pizzey 1974, p. 48).

Lucy, 24, went to the centre with her two small children. She had married the man of her dreams but " ... days after she married him, he lost his temper over some shirts she'd forgotten to iron and he beat her up. She had black eyes and a broken nose" (p. 38). Like many battered women, Lucy said that she still loved her husband but hated the beatings (p. 40).

Jocelynne Scutt's *Even in the Best of Homes: Violence in the Family* (1983), based on the case histories of 312 participants, provides overwhelming evidence of abuse suffered by women and children. Written from a legal perspective, Scutt's study was an important contribution to the feminist agenda of uncovering the truth about the extent of men's violence against women in the home and the inadequacy of police and legal responses. Courageously confronting her own profession, she said that until

... fairness extends to both women and men then discrimination through the legal system will continue to ensure that women who are victims of domestic violence find little help in the process of going to court (Scutt 1983, p. 259).

In the United States, Ellen Pence was a pioneer in the field of domestic violence. As a feminist and social activist, her interest lay in developing an effective plan that would keep women safe and, at the same time, work with violent men to change their behaviour. She and a few of her colleagues in Duluth, Minnesota, created the Domestic Abuse Intervention Program, known the world over as the Duluth Model, in the early 1980s.

Put simply, the aims of the Duluth Model, which still informs the work done by feminist domestic and family violence services everywhere, are: keep victims safe; don't blame victims for the abuse; and hold abusers accountable for their actions.[18]

Pence and one of her colleagues worked with women's groups exploring the dynamics of men's violence against women and out of those discussions came the Power and Control Wheel – a tool which sets out in unapologetic terms the tactics perpetrators use to maintain power and control over their victims. The Power and Control Wheel is unmatched in its ability to help victims and perpetrators understand the dynamics when men are violent. The hope was that an understanding of a violent man's behaviour would be the first step in him deciding to change his behaviour.

Ellen Pence co-authored two publications – with Michael Paymar, *Educational Groups for Men Who Batter: The Duluth Model* (Pence and Paymar 1993), and with Melanie F. Shepard, *Coordinated Community Response to Domestic Violence: Lessons from the Duluth Model* (Shepard and Pence 1999).

Today, as in the early days of Second Wave feminism, feminists continue in their determination to expose the truth about men's violence against women in the home, stressing the need for governments to address the political, social and economic inequalities that privilege men and enable men's violence against women (Hanmer and Itzin (Eds) 2001; McLellan 1999/2006; Batty with Corbett 2016; Hill 2019 and 2021).

All of these areas were highlighted by Second Wave feminists as needing a massive injection of truth. Society's insistence on ignoring and/or minimising the harms done to women by pornography, prostitution, sexual assault, surrogacy and domestic violence reveals a yawning gap that can only be remedied by honest and ethical leadership in the political sphere.

In addition, Second Wave feminists explored and wrote about discrimination on the basis of sex, the use of language,

---

18 <https://www.theduluthmodel.org>.

the silencing and attempted erasure of women, freedom of speech, globalisation, justice, education, employment, war and peace, nuclear proliferation and much more – with the aim of uncovering the truth about patriarchal dominance. Here I will highlight the work done in just three of those areas: discrimination on the basis of sex, the use of language and, more recently, the attempted erasure of women.

Discrimination on the basis of sex

In exploring the reasons behind the imbalance of power between the sexes, feminists pointed to the influence of sexual stereotyping. Girls and boys are born into a world where they learn through socialisation what is expected of them. Simone de Beauvoir wrote that girls learn that they are the 'second sex', forced into second place in relation to boys.

After quoting Aristotle who said "we should regard the female nature as afflicted with a natural defectiveness," and St Thomas Aquinas who pronounced woman to be an "imperfect man," an "incidental being," de Beauvoir went on to say:

> Thus humanity is male and man defines woman not in herself but relative to him; she is not regarded as an autonomous being ...
>
> She is defined and differentiated with reference to man and not he with reference to her; she is the incidental, the inessential as opposed to the essential. He is the Subject, he is the Absolute – she is the Other (de Beauvoir 1953, p. 16).

Throughout her book, she develops this argument:

> One is not born, but rather becomes a woman ...
>
> Up to the age of twelve the little girl is as strong as her brothers, and she shows the same mental powers ... but ... the influence of others upon the child is a factor almost from the start, and thus she is indoctrinated with her vocation from her earliest years (pp. 295–296).

CHAPTER ONE: FEMINIST FOCUS ON TRUTH AND TRUTH-TELLING

Betty Friedan wrote in 1963 about "The Problem that Has No Name." Never spoken about was "a strange stirring, a sense of dissatisfaction, a yearning that women suffered in the middle of the twentieth century in the United States," she said. Among many other things, women were taught

> ... how to dress, look, and act more feminine and make marriage more exciting; how to keep their husbands from dying young and their sons from growing into delinquents. They were taught to pity the neurotic, unfeminine, unhappy women who wanted to be poets or physicists or presidents. They learned that truly feminine women do not want careers, higher education, political rights ... (Friedan 1963, p. 13).

This yearning, this "nameless aching dissatisfaction" (p. 30), existed as a result of the rigid sex-role stereotyping that Friedan and other early Second Wave feminists were beginning to name.

Shulamith Firestone begins her feminist classic *The Dialectic of Sex* with the words: "Sex class is so deep as to be invisible." On that basis, she refers to Second Wave feminism as "the most important revolution in history" and says:

> Its aim: overthrow of the oldest, most rigid class/caste system in existence, the class system based on sex – a system consolidated over thousands of years, lending the archetypal male and female roles an undeserved legitimacy and seeming permanence (Firestone 1970, p. 23).

Germaine Greer called for a feminist revolution:

> The revolutionary woman must know her enemies, the doctors, psychiatrists, health visitors, priests, marriage counsellors, policemen, magistrates and genteel reformers, all the authoritarians and dogmatists who flock about her with warnings and advice. She must know her friends, her sisters, and seek in their lineaments her own. With them she can discover co-operation, sympathy and love (Greer 1971, pp. 19–20).

Greer spoke of marriage as a patriarchal trap for women. "If independence is a necessary concomitant of freedom," she wrote, "women must not marry" (p. 32). A woman "must recapture her own will and her own goals, and the energy to use them ..." (p. 323).

As a socialist feminist contemplating revolution, she painted a picture of socialism and feminism working together:

> ... we cannot argue that all will be well when the socialists have succeeded in abolishing private property and restoring public ownership of the means of production. We cannot wait that long. Women's liberation, if it abolishes the patriarchal family, will abolish a necessary substructure of the authoritarian state, and once that withers away Marx will have come true willy-nilly, so let's get on with it (pp. 328–329).

Kate Millett referred to patriarchy's system of sexual relationship as "a relationship of dominance and subordinance," and pointed out:

> What goes largely unexamined, often even unacknowledged ... in our social order, is the birthright priority whereby males rule females. Through this system a most ingenious form of 'interior colonization' has been achieved (Millett 1970, p. 25).

Anne Summers illustrated de Beauvoir's claim that "man defines woman not in herself but relative to him" when she wrote her first book *Damned Whores and God's Police* (Summers 1975).

Feminists have been the first to recognise and admit that discrimination based on sex has a negative effect on men as well as on women. There has been very little appetite on the part of men to examine those negative effects and one can only guess the reason. On the one hand, very few men would want to question a system that ascribes power and privilege to their sex for fear of losing it and, on the other hand, more powerful men would not want to interfere with a system that allows them to exploit those men who are less powerful, so that the wheels of patriarchy can keep turning in favour of the powerful. One man who has been willing to look honestly at the effect sex discrimination has on men is Robert Jensen in his 2017 book *The End of Patriarchy: Radical Feminism for Men* (Jensen 2017).

Kathleen Barry, American sociologist and radical feminist, who had courageously analysed and exposed the truth about international human sex trafficking in the 1970s (Barry 1979) and written extensively on the negative effects of prostitution and pornography in the 1990s (Barry 1995), turned her attention in the early years of the new millennium to the disastrous effects of war. Of her 2010 book, *Unmaking War, Remaking Men*, she says: "(T)his book focuses directly on the masculinity of war ... from how masculinity is made to how militaries turn men into remorseless killers ..." She objects strongly to the "dehumanization of men" that occurs when soldiers are preparing for combat, and to their "expendability," illustrated by the fact that they are sent off to war knowing that they could die. In every warmongering country, the way boys are socialised is intended to prepare them for war, Barry says, and continues:

> Our societies impose powerful negative sanctions on men who refuse violent masculinity. Boys who are not aggressive, who cower when attacked by other boys, and who will not fight, are bullied and taunted for being wimps and wusses. Those men who are caring, soft and tender risk ridicule for being effeminate, that is, like a woman (Barry 2010, p. 17).

For wars to be "unmade," Barry argues, there must first be a "remaking" of the way society characterises masculinity.

Language

Discrimination on the basis of sex is aided and abetted by the many ways in which language is used in the service of patriarchy, as early Second Wave feminists were quick to point out.

Naming

Naming is one of the ways language was used and misused. In *Beyond God the Father* (1973), Mary Daly focused attention on the importance of naming and sought to reveal the truth. She said:

> ... it is necessary to grasp the fundamental fact that women have had the power of *naming* stolen from us. We have not been free to use our own power to name ourselves, the world, or God ... (Daly 1973, p. 8).

She called on women to reclaim the right to name: "The liberation of language is rooted in the liberation of ourselves." To illustrate that point in a powerful way, Daly wrote:

> As aliens in a man's world who are now rising up to name – that is, to create – our own world, women are beginning to recognize that the value system that has been thrust upon us by the various cultural institutions of patriarchy has amounted to a kind of gang rape of minds as well as bodies (p. 9).

Andrea Dworkin included "the power of naming" when she listed all the ways men have exercised power over women. She said:

> ... men have the power of naming, a great and sublime power. This power of naming enables men to define experience, to articulate boundaries and values, to designate to each thing its realm and qualities, to determine what can and cannot be expressed, to control perception itself (Dworkin 1979, p. 17).

Phyllis Chesler, in her devastatingly honest book, *Women and Madness*, brought to light the ways in which psychiatry has labelled and manipulated and enslaved women throughout history. Women who constantly experience depression because of the powerlessness of their lives, generally find themselves seeking some kind of psychiatric intervention: medication or hospitalisation. The focus of the medical/psychiatric profession, Chesler maintained, is almost always on the patient herself rather than on the circumstances of her life that may have caused her sense of powerlessness (Chesler 1972).

Patriarchy names women who express their disappointment and disillusionment with the female role as 'difficult'; women who no longer want to have sex with their partner as 'frigid'; women who freely express their anger as 'out of control'; women who report their partner's violence to police as 'guilty of provoking him'; and so on. When women take back the power of naming, they counter the dishonesty that has worked to keep them powerless. By doing their own naming, they take back the power to make decisions for themselves and their world.

Silencing

Silencing was another important focus of Second Wave feminists. Just as the power of naming was stolen from women, so was the power that comes from speaking out and being heard. Radical political feminists sought to sift through the lies and reveal the truth about the silencing of women.

Adrienne Rich wrote about "the erasure of women's political and historic past." Each generation of feminist thinkers and activists are made to disappear from history, giving the impression that there may be individual 'trouble-makers' in each generation but no feminist tradition:

> The entire history of women's struggle for self-determination has been muffled in silence over and over. One serious cultural obstacle encountered by any feminist writer is that each feminist work has tended to be received as if it emerged

from nowhere; as if each of us had lived, thought, and worked without any historical past or contextual present (Rich 1979, pp. 9–11).

Dale Spender continued this theme in *Women of Ideas (And What Men Have Done to Them)* when she wrote:

> Women's experience is non-existent, invisible, unreal from the outset, and it is my contention that if patriarchy is to be preserved, women's invisibility must remain. Obviously, this is not, for me, a state to be desired (Spender 1982, p. 9).

Spender proceeded to research the lives and work of women from Aphra Behn to Adrienne Rich with a view to bringing them back into view.

Other books have been written pointing out the silencing of women that occurs in personal and social situations. Prior to *Women of Ideas*, Dale Spender had written *Man Made Language* (1980) in which she describes the way women's silence has been constructed so that men's voices will always have dominance. In a chapter titled: 'The Dominant and the Muted', Spender writes:

> Women are muted because men are in control and the language, and the meanings, and the knowledge of women cannot be accounted for outside that male control. If women's meanings are to have unfettered impression, then it seems that men must cease to have control (Spender 1980, p. 77).

Being silenced is an all-too-common experience for women, both at home and in the workplace. For example, many women have testified to the fact that a suggestion they made in a committee meeting or staff meeting was totally ignored, only to be regurgitated by a male colleague a few minutes later with quite a different response. *His* idea is praised and taken up by all in attendance. And what of the woman? She is left with a feeling of unreality. "Am I here? Did I speak? Was it my fault? My tone of voice? My choice of words?" No, it was simply because she is a woman and women's voices are muted, silenced, ignored.

Obscurantism

Obscurantism was exposed by Second Wave feminists as another tactic of patriarchy in the same way that earlier waves of women activists had pointed to language being used to create a false reality. While the American constitution said that "... all men are created equal" and women were assured that the word 'men' included women, the Declaration of Sentiments produced at the Seneca Falls Women's Convention in 1848, began with the words: "We hold these truths to be self-evident; that all men and women are created equal ... " In every generation, when feminists have raised the issue of male language, they have been assured that 'men' means 'men and women', 'he' means 'he and she', 'his' means 'his and hers', and so on. But the reality has always been that, in practice, women are excluded.

The relationship between man and God is an obvious example. Women have been assured that 'man was made in the image of God' actually meant 'man and woman' but, in the Judeo-Christian tradition, God the Father is clearly male, Jesus the Son is clearly male and, the pronouns used for the Holy Spirit indicate that the third person of the Trinity is also male. This led feminists to suggest that God was made in the image of man rather than the other way around.

According to Dale Spender, the use of language to confuse and deceive interferes with our ability to understand the world as it is:

> Language is our means of classifying and ordering the world: our means of manipulating reality. In its structure and in its use we bring our world into realization, and if it is inherently inaccurate, then we are misled. If the rules which underlie our

language system, our symbolic order, are invalid, then we are daily deceived (1980, pp. 2–3).

Postmodern theory, variously criticised as self-contradictory, incoherent and nihilistic, is a classic example of a theory that encourages the use of language to confuse. Its attempt to rationalise feminism provoked fierce criticism from Somer Brodribb:

> I define poststructuralism/postmodernism as a neurotic symptom and scene of repression of women's claims for truth and justice. Postmodernism is the attempted masculine ir/rationalization of feminism (Brodribb 1992, p. 20).

She called it "this masculinity *in extremis*, this masculine liberal philosophy in totalitarian form" (p. 20).

Denise Thompson illustrated this by highlighting "postmodernism's inability to challenge structures of domination," thereby rendering the idea of a post modern feminism a contradiction in terms:

> While feminism needs to be able to identify domination in general, and male domination in particular, in order to challenge it, post-modernism refuses to identify, and hence cannot contest, relations of domination and subordination (Thompson 1996, p. 325).

Susan Hawthorne, in her 2004 essay 'The political uses of obscurantism', reminded us: "Language has its political uses and obscure language is always helpful to those in power." She demonstrates the way postmodern interventions in language have served patriarchy at the expense of feminism's calls for truth and clarity.

In response to the strength of Second Wave feminism, postmodernism sought to shore up patriarchy's power by changing the language and encouraging the use of words that would be more palatable to men. But terms like 'gender', 'gender mainstreaming' and 'intersectionality' with their 'intentional neutrality' are deliberately depoliticising, said Hawthorne. It was for that same reason, no doubt, that American feminist bell hooks preferred to spell out the multitude of oppressions rather than use the catch-all word 'intersectionality'. Her preference for using the term "imperialist white-supremacist capitalist patriarchy" left no doubt about the power imbalances needing to be addressed (hooks, 2013).

Hawthorne went on to discuss other examples of obscurantism. Women's Studies and Feminist Studies programs, she said, became Gender Studies or Cultural Studies. The words Lesbian and Gay became Queer and LGBTI (with more letters added in subsequent years). Feminist research and language were appropriated, watered down, and used to undermine feminist projects:

> In the process, the original ideas are watered down to a point where they are no longer recognisable as political demands for social justice. They are simply mechanisms for keeping rowdy people – especially women – quiet.

Hawthorne concludes her article with a call to action:

> Politicians and bureaucrats revel in obscurantism and one of the powerful challenges to this is sheer clarity of language. Obscurantism leads to political passivity and social fatalism. Feminists need always to be awake to such strategies and the use of clear, context specific and direct language is the first step in truly transforming society (Hawthorne 2004).

Attempted erasure of women

As women's courage grew in the early years of Second Wave feminism and protests became louder and more determined, patriarchal forces were at a loss to know how to respond. First, they began co-opting some of the language of the feminist uprising. Words like 'empowerment' and 'assertiveness' were taken out of the language of the collective and presented as goals that individual women could aim for. Slogans focusing on individual women's achievements like *Women can do anything* took the place of *Sisterhood is powerful* and *Break the silence on domestic violence*. Placing the emphasis on what individual women could achieve with a little bit of effort on their part conveniently took the focus off the system that was designed to give men power and privilege over women. The aim was to keep women focused on themselves rather than on the system that oppressed them.

It was clear, however, that patriarchy was shaken by the strength of feminist protests. Not satisfied with taking over feminist words and slogans and remaking them to fit their own agenda, patriarchy moved into a phase that had the potential to erase women altogether. In the introduction to *The Transsexual Empire* (1979), Janice G. Raymond made this observation:

> Given the historical difficulties in molding both female flesh and energy to patriarchal standards, an alternative is to make the biological woman obsolete by the creation of man-made 'she-males' (Raymond 1979, p. xvii).

In this important book, Raymond exposed the powerful entities working to support men and women who express a desire to transition to the other sex:

> What we witness in the transsexual context is a number of medical specialties combining to create transsexuals – urologists, gynaecologists, endocrinologists, plastic surgeons and the like (p. xv).

Added to this list are speech therapists, drug companies, psychiatrists and psychologists, all working to create what Raymond calls "artifactual femaleness … constructed, fashioned, and fabricated" (p. xvi).

In the introduction to the second edition of *The Transsexual Empire* in 1994, Janice G. Raymond reiterates her concern for the suffering some transsexuals experience and blames the medical and psychological industries for giving them false hope:

> I accept the fact that transsexuals have suffered an enormous amount of physical and emotional pain. But I don't accept the fact that someone's *desire* to be a woman, or a man, makes one a woman or man. Or that the instrumentality of hormones and surgery creates a real woman or man (Raymond 1994, p. xxiv).

Jennifer Bilek, a New York-based investigative journalist and author of the *11th Hour* blog, agrees. In her writing about transgenderism (which she prefers to call "synthetic sex identities"), she exposes the billionaires behind the transgender agenda, and the many universities and medical/psychological entities in the United States and other countries that have gladly accepted the money on offer and set up gender clinics to support men, women and children in their quest to transition to the other sex (Bilek 2022; Bilek 2024).

An important comparison is being made between transgenderism and eugenics. "Transgenderism is a eugenics project," wrote Jennifer Bilek, "driven by Big Pharma, the state, and billionaires in order to engineer human sexual evolution" (Bilek 2021).

Other significant feminist writers and commentators warning of the attempted erasure of women include: Sheila Jeffreys (*Gender Hurts: A Feminist Analysis of the Politics of Transgenderism*, 2014; also *Penile Imperialism: The Male Sex Right and Women's Subordination*, 2022); Janice G. Raymond (*Doublethink: A Feminist Challenge to Transgenderism*, 2021); Heather Brunskell-Evans (*Transgender Body Politics*, 2020); Meghan Murphy (*Feminist Current* website, section on Gender, 2012 to the present); and many others.

As an exercise in truth-discovery and truth-telling, the work of Second Wave feminists in the latter part of the twentieth century and into the twenty-first century, is unsurpassed. And while patriarchy has done all it can to question and delegitimise radical feminist analysis, the fact is that the courage of those early feminists lit a flame for women and that flame continues burning to this day. The tradition of truth-telling and confronting lies and disinformation is still front and centre of the feminist endeavour, as I will illustrate in the next chapter.

CHAPTER TWO

Speaking Truth to Power

The courage demonstrated by early radical feminists has instilled in women and girls of subsequent generations a belief that they have a right and, indeed, an obligation to speak out about all of the ways they and their friends are disempowered, violated and abused under patriarchy.

Since the turn of the millennium, societies around the world have been stunned by the numbers of women speaking out and revealing their experiences of abuse by men of their acquaintance and virtually shouting from the rooftops: 'ENOUGH IS ENOUGH'. Their courage and, some would say, audacity, speaks volumes about their determination to create a better, safer world for women and girls.

A stand-out initiative is the #MeToo movement initiated in 2006 by Tarana Burke. Born in the Bronx, New York, in 1973, she was a victim/survivor of sexual assault and rape as a child and a teenager. In 2006, she began using the term 'MeToo' on social media to empower other women of colour to speak out about their abuse.

In 2015, Ambra Gutierrez, a 22-year-old Italian model accused American film producer, Harvey Weinstein, of touching her inappropriately. The New York City Police Department (NYPD) believed her and progressed their investigation but, as soon as the accusations became public, the right-wing media turned the story around and accused Gutierrez of lying. Subsequently, the District Attorney decided not to proceed with charges against Weinstein.

In 2016, Ukrainian journalist Anastasia Melnichenko posted on social media inviting people to tell their personal stories of sexual abuse and harassment. Thousands of women and some men in both Russia and Ukraine began posting their experiences of abuse using the hashtag #IAmNotAfraidToSay.[19]

Then, in 2017, following more accusations against Harvey Weinstein, actor Alyssa Milano wrote on Twitter inviting her followers to respond with "me too" if they had been sexually assaulted or harassed. The response was overwhelming. The very next day, Milano was made aware of the earlier #MeToo movement, gave credit to Tarana Burke and provided a link to her website. With that, the #MeToo movement took off again and several high-profile men have been called to answer for their alleged sexual abuse of women.[20]

As the movement progressed and more and more women added their voices, another initiative called 'TIME'S UP' was launched in January 2018 by several of Hollywood's high-profile women. In an open letter to *The New York Times* and the Spanish-language newspaper *La Opinión*, the signatories stated that their goal was to support women who chose to bring charges against their perpetrators. They set up the TIME'S UP

---

19 RT News, 9 July 2016. '#I Am Not Afraid to Say: Thousands of Sexual Violence Victims Share Harrowing Stories on Facebook'. <https://www.rt.com/news/350338-sexual-violence-online-flashmob/>.

20 By 31 October 2017, more than 80 women had come forward alleging sexual harassment or rape against Harvey Weinstein (Williams 2017). Following his arrest in New York in 2018, he was found guilty of rape and sentenced to 23 years in prison (Ranson 2020). In 2021, he was extradited to Los Angeles to face further charges that resulted in his being sentenced to a further 16 years' imprisonment, to be served following his New York sentence (Queally 2023). <https://metoomvmt.org>.

Legal Defense Fund that in the first week of its existence raised almost $15 million. By October 2018, it had risen to $22 million. TIME'S UP also had an advocacy arm to push for the creation of laws to protect women and punish companies that ignore complaints of sexual harassment. A decision was made to wind up operations in January 2023 and move the funds of TIME'S UP to the National Women's Law Centre in Washington.[21]

When the Movement was established, the TIME'S UP website stated that the organisation had three goals:

Safety
We demand that every person is free from sexual harassment, assault, retaliation, and other forms of discrimination on the job. Period.

Equity
Everyone deserves a fair shot at success. Let's level the playing field for working women of all kinds.

Power
Sexual harassment is about power – who has it, who doesn't, and the deep imbalance that has persisted for far too long. We're challenging the status quo.

Separate from #MeToo and TIME'S UP was another initiative aimed at raising awareness of the harassment women live with every day. It was the Everyday Sexism Project introduced by Laura Bates in 2012. Bates set up a website and invited women and girls to tell of their experiences of sexism. A decade later, entries are still being posted (almost every day) on the website, by email and on Twitter (now called X). The invitation on the website reads:

The Everyday Sexism Project exists to catalogue instances of sexism experienced by women on a day to day basis ...

---

21 <https://www.abc.net.au/news/2023-01-22/times-up-metoo-group-halts-operations/101880136>.

> Say as much or as little as you like, use your real name or a pseudonym – it's up to you. By sharing your story you're showing the world that sexism does exist, it is faced by women everyday and it is a valid problem to discuss.[22]

When truth is told, as in #MeToo, TIME'S UP and the Everyday Sexism Project, patriarchy shudders and perpetrators of unethical and criminal practices run for cover.[23] Women who lay charges against their abusers often pay a heavy price as all the forces of patriarchy line up against them, but women remain determined to do it.

In recent times, Australia has experienced an outpouring of truth as women challenge men's sense of entitlement and speak out about the sexual abuse, harassment and rape they have endured over many years.

Women's courage rose out of the rage all women felt when hearing the testimony of a young woman, Brittany Higgins, that she had been raped in 2018 on the couch in a government minister's office in Parliament House, by a man who was a staff member in that same minister's office. Initially, the story was hushed up and Brittany transferred to a different office. Two years later, however, the story broke as Brittany Higgins agreed to be interviewed by award-winning journalist Samantha Maiden.

As she tells it, Brittany, who was a junior staff member, had enjoyed a night out with other staffers, had drunk too much, and had accepted a ride home by a fellow worker whom she trusted. Instead of driving her home he took her, in the early hours of the morning, to the minister's office in Parliament House. Security guards had no qualms about letting them in because they both had security clearance. Brittany alleges that she fell

---

22 Everyday Sexism Project. <everydaysexism.com>.
23 Running for cover can take the form of blaming the victim, attacking the messenger, suing for defamation or just being quiet in an effort to make oneself a small target.

into an alcohol-induced sleep and woke up on the couch with her male companion raping her. He quickly exited the building, leaving Brittany naked on the couch where a security guard subsequently found her.

Following that experience, Brittany Higgins knew that if she kept quiet about the incident she would be able to continue working in the job she loved in Parliament House, so that is what she did. But the awful effects of what happened never left her. Eventually, she resigned from her job and, after giving it much thought, decided to speak out about her experience.

At about the same time, the truth about an historic rape began to surface, pointing the finger at the then Attorney-General of Australia, Christian Porter. The accusation was that, in 1988, he brutally raped a friend when she was 16 and he 17, an accusation that he strongly denies. The woman, who is referred to as Kate, struggled throughout her life until, in 2019, she began pouring out her story to friends. One of her friends wrote to the Prime Minister Scott Morrison, attaching a copy of a detailed statement prepared by Kate for her lawyer. Copies were also sent to Labor Senator Penny Wong and Greens Senator Sarah Hanson-Young who both forwarded the letter and statement to the Australian Federal Police.

While an investigation would be complicated by the fact that, after Kate engaged a lawyer, told many friends and spoke with the New South Wales Police, she then took her own life, women all around the country were angry at the thought that this, too, would be swept under the carpet. Women insisted that, since the accused was a senior minister in the government, it would be even more urgent that the matter be investigated and justice be done.

These two matters, the truth-telling by Brittany Higgins and Kate, emboldened other women to come out and tell their stories of the sexual abuse they had suffered at the hands of men, both inside Parliament House and within the wider community: work colleagues, so-called friends and acquaintances. Indeed, one young woman, Chanel Contos, reflecting on her own and her friends' experiences, started a petition calling for 'consent' to be included in sex education in schools and opened up a space in social media for high school girls to discuss their experiences. One international newspaper reported that the petition attracted 21,804 signatories, and more than 4000 girls responded with stories of rape and sexual abuse by high school boys.[24] As the weeks went by, the numbers grew. Looking back on the action, Contos reported in December 2021 that when her original petition developed into "a national campaign demanding consent education," it attracted more than 45,000 signatures. Also, she reported, there were "more than 6,700 people who named the school that their perpetrator of sexual assault went to" (Contos 2021).

Not surprisingly, the response from some high school boys was immediate. Journalist Madonna King described the response as: "Hate to the accusers delivered by Instagram. Accusations by Snapchat. Threats by text." In addition, she referred to a "revolting episode unfolding at Villanova College in [the Brisbane suburb of] Coorparoo where students have been involved in sickening, misogynist online videos ... "[25] The outpouring of truth by Australian women and girls coincided with the naming of a young woman, Grace Tame, as Australian of the Year 2021. Grace told her story of having been groomed at

---

24 GCT Team. 2 March 2021. 'Viral Petition by Chanel Contos: 4000+ People Come Forward with Allegations of Sexual Assault'. *Greek City Times*. <https://greekcitytimes.com/2021/03/02/petition-contos-sexual-assault/>.
25 Madonna King, 20 May 2021, 'Boys to Men: The "Epidemic" Infecting Our Nation That's Not Being Taken Seriously', *In Queensland*. <https://inqld.com.au/opinion/2021/05/20/boys-to-men-theres-another-epidemic-infecting-our-nation-and-its-not-being-taken-seriously/>.

CHAPTER TWO: SPEAKING TRUTH TO POWER

15 years of age and used for sex by her 58-year-old high school maths teacher, Nicolaas Ockert Bester, who committed 20 to 30 sexual assaults against her.[26] She spoke of her struggle with anorexia and other mental health issues following the abuse, and of the years of therapy that helped her, finally, to understand what had happened to her and find her way back to health.

Grace's courage, together with her determination that Australians confront the issue of sexual abuse, has helped other women find their voices.

When the call went out for women and men to join March4Justice protests on 15 March 2021, immediately there were marches and rallies organised in over 100 cities and towns. In Melbourne, 5000 people marched. Similarly, other capital cities and regional towns and cities saw women out in force. While many politicians joined the marches in a show of solidarity with the estimated 110,000 who marched nationally, the Prime Minister Scott Morrison, the Minister for Women Marise Payne, and others in the government of the day ran for cover. In a move obviously designed to retain some power in the situation, the Prime Minister invited organisers to meet him in his office but his invitation was declined, and he was left to ponder his next move.

Grace Tame had urged women: "Speak your truth. It is your power." By joining the protest marches, women all around Australia were speaking their truth and feeling their power.

The Prime Minister's next move (which was appreciated by all fair-minded Australians) was to ask Sex Discrimination Commissioner, Kate Jenkins, to conduct a review:

---

26   Nina Funnell, 22 August 2019, '#LetHerSpeak: Monster Hiding in Plain Sight – Grace Tame's Sexual Abuse Ordeal Revealed', *News.com.au*. <https://www.news.com.au/lifestyle/real-life/monster-hiding-in-plain-sight-grace-tames-repulsive-schoolgirl-sexual-abuse-ordeal-revealed/news-story/12de77bdf1a2170975b0ef1 02dd3c59e>.

On 5 March 2021, the Independent Review into Commonwealth Parliamentary Workplaces (Review) was established by the Australian Government, with support from the Federal Opposition and crossbench. Conducted by the Australian Human Rights Commission and led by the Sex Discrimination Commissioner, the Review was asked to make recommendations to ensure that Commonwealth parliamentary workplaces are safe and respectful and that the nation's Parliament reflects best practice in prevention and response to bullying, sexual harassment and sexual assault.[27]

The report, *Set the Standard: Report on the Independent Review into Commonwealth Parliamentary Workplaces* was tabled on 30 November 2021 following the analysis of contributions from 1723 individuals and 33 organisations and collectives. It names the drivers of bullying, sexual harassment and sexual assault as a misuse of power; gender inequality; lack of accountability; and a sense of entitlement in some groups, and marginalisation and exclusion of others.[28]

The report concludes with 28 recommendations designed to assist the government in bringing about the kinds of changes that are now being demanded by women and men alike.

Prior to the establishment of the review, one cohort of women who enabled the awful truths revealed by Brittany Higgins, Grace Tame and Kate to reach the ears and eyes of the general public was a group of journalists who saw their role in a democracy as that of reporting and commenting on issues as truthfully as they could. While they represented various media organisations, they nevertheless appeared to be of one mind in supporting the

---

[27] Australian Human Rights Commission, 30 November 2021, 'Set the Standard: Report on the Independent Review into Commonwealth Parliamentary Workplaces (2021)'. <https://humanrights.gov.au/set-standard-2021>.

[28] <https://humanrights.gov.au/sites/default/files/2021-11/ahrc_set_the_standard_report_executive_summary_2021.pdf>.

truth-tellers and questioning the 'nothing to see here' attitude of the government.

In an extraordinary article aimed at shooting the messenger, *The Australian Financial Review*'s senior correspondent Aaron Patrick attacked the political editor of news.com.au, Samantha Maiden, who had interviewed Brittany Higgins and enabled her to reveal the allegation that she had been raped in a minister's office in Parliament House. Samantha Maiden stood firm, and numerous people came out in support of her: #IStandWithSam. In the same article, Patrick named other women journalists and accused them of straying into "unapologetic activism":

> Angry coverage that often strayed into unapologetic activism came forth from a new, female media leadership: Laura Tingle and Louise Milligan on the ABC, Katharine Murphy and Amy Remeikis at the Guardian, Lisa Wilkinson on Channel Ten, Karen Middleton in the Saturday Paper and a cameo by Jessica Irvine on the Nine Network (Patrick 2021).

His article, supported by his editor-in-chief Michael Stutchbury, was condemned by journalists from across the media. As Amanda Meade wrote for *The Guardian*, their "hit job" backfired spectacularly (Meade 2021).

Whenever anyone speaks truth to power, the truth-teller can pay a heavy price, as was the case when Brittany Higgins made the decision to report her rape to police and pursue charges against her alleged rapist, Bruce Lehrmann.

The trial was a classic example of how rape cases generally proceed in Australia. At first, the Australian Federal Police were reluctant to bring charges against Lehrmann and pushed back against pressure from the Department of Public Prosecutions (DPP). Then, when charges were laid and the trial began, it was as though the alleged victim herself was on trial. Brittany Higgins was questioned, ridiculed and accused of lying by defence lawyers. She was forced to defend herself day after day, while the accused simply claimed his right not to take the stand and remain silent.

After 12 gruelling days, the trial was aborted due to the misconduct of one of the jurors. Following expert medical advice that a second trial would pose a "significant and unacceptable risk" to Higgins' mental health, the prosecutor announced that the case would not be proceeding. So, after Brittany Higgins was put on trial for 12 days, there was no actual result for her efforts ... except mental anguish and pain. Bruce Lehrmann, on the other hand, has proceeded to sue media outlets, for defamation.[29]

In the case of Kate, the accused also began defamation proceedings against the media. Australia's ex-Attorney-General, Christian Porter's immediate response was to sue the ABC and journalist Louise Milligan for a report that Porter believed pointed to him as the rapist, even though the ABC was careful not to mention names.[30]

A note about defamation

A common feature in cases where women speak out about violence against them is the use of the law of defamation by the accused.

Jennifer Robinson and Keina Yoshida, in Chapter 6 of their book *How Many More Women?: Exposing How the Law Silences*

---

[29] Following the aborted trial and the decision not to proceed with a new trial, an emboldened Bruce Lehrmann sued Network Ten and presenter Lisa Wilkinson for defamation. The evidence, however, proved Network Ten's truth defence and Lehrmann's defamation claim failed. Justice Michael Lee found, on the balance of probabilities, that "Mr Lehrmann raped Ms Higgins." <https://www.abc.net.au/news/2024-04-15/bruce-lehrmann-defamation-trial-judgment/103706656>.

[30] Realising his case would be difficult to prove, Porter subsequently dropped the defamation case. No damages were paid by the ABC and, following mediation, the ABC agreed to attach a note to the online article stating that they had not intended to suggest that Mr Porter had committed the alleged criminal offences and regretted that some readers may have interpreted the article in that way.

Women, focus on the law of defamation and indicate that it is "always a question of weighing his right to reputation against her right to free speech" (p. 297), but it is rarely a level playing field. After many examples of women being silenced, they conclude their discussion by saying:

> The law of defamation has been weaponised by rich and powerful men to silence women who might speak out against them. Women speaking out and journalists reporting their stories cannot afford to defend the cases – and their freedom of speech. This must be acknowledged and made right (p. 296).

⟨◈⟩

Those involved in the early years of the radical feminist revolution known as Second Wave feminism observe the courage of women like Brittany Higgins, Grace Tame, Chanel Contos and all who spoke out publicly on #MeToo, and identify a sameness and continuity with the values and passion of those early feminists. Today's young feminist activists also acknowledge the continuity. When celebrating the enormity of the 2021 March4Justice protests, Chanel Contos wrote: "We leveraged the work of human rights activists and feminists for generations before us so that those after us can do the same" (Contos 2021). Women today are rising up and demonstrating that they are not afraid to speak and insisting that they will continue speaking out till they are heard. Such determination appears to be coming out of women's exasperation over all the ways that men in power find, bolstered by the patriarchal institutions that support them, to avoid the truth.

In addition to all the truth-telling by those whose lives have been affected by sexual abuse and harassment, there is the rise in Australia of strong women journalists. Also, we are seeing the rise of independent politicians. Women, mostly moderate liberals who despair at the increasingly conservative agenda of the Liberal party, stood as independent candidates in the 2022 federal election and had considerable success on election day. This movement away from the major political parties toward independents gained influential supporters. Retired politicians from both sides of politics as well as high-profile business leaders spoke out in support of independents (both women and men) believing it was the only way to shock major political parties into a confrontation with reality. Politics in Australia had descended into a joust between two sides, no holds barred, and the general public were sick and tired of the lies, the gotcha moments and the lack of accountability. It appeared to observers of politics that the concerns of the community came second to the fight between politicians to hold on to or gain power.

The women who offered themselves up for election as independents pointed to their frustration at the lack of action over many years on issues such as climate change, cruel treatment of asylum-seekers, men's physical and sexual abuse of women, as well as the need for an independent body to deal with corruption when it occurs in politics, government departments and statutory bodies.

Another phenomenon that reveals the effect of Second Wave feminism on societies around the world is the fact that very young women, indeed schoolgirls, are standing up and speaking their truth about the need for climate action. Greta Thunberg, born in Stockholm, Sweden in 2003, was the undisputed leader of the worldwide campaign among school children for climate action. In Australia, also, it is still mainly girls and young women who are taking the lead as they work together with boys for a better future.

Anjali Sharma, an Indian-born Australian high school student became so concerned about the effects of climate change that she started an Instagram account and spent a year "ranting about climate change" to her 12,000 followers. During and after the unprecedented bushfires of 2020, she became aware that many teenagers shared her concerns. Next she joined the School Strike for Climate movement and became one of the organisers in her area (Perkins 2021).

Then, at the age of 16, Anjali became the lead litigant in a class action against the federal government, asking the Federal Court to stop the then Minister for the Environment, Sussan Ley, from approving an expansion of the Vickery coalmine in New South Wales, on the basis that she had a duty of care toward future generations. In the case *Sharma & Others v Minister for the Environment*, Judge Mordecai Bromberg of the Federal Court of Australia ruled that the minister did have a duty of care. The nine teenagers involved in the class action were Anjali Sharma, Isolde Shanti Raj-Seppings, Ambrose Malachy Hayes, Tomas Webster Arbizu, Bella Paige Burgemeister, Laura Fleck Kirwan, Ava Princi, Veronica Hester and Luca Gwyther Saunders. Because all applicants were under the age of 18, they were joined by a litigation representative, Sister Marie Brigid Arthur.

The group was elated at the decision but then devastated when, in March 2022, the case was overturned on appeal by the Full Court of the Federal Court. Anjali Sharma wrote: "It feels like we didn't just lose a court case … It feels like we've lost our chance to push the government further on the climate crisis, and with it, lost our chance for a safe future." With what seems like a promise to rise from the ashes of defeat, however, she goes on to say: "I'm trying to act strong. I'm trying to speak from the heart and reassure everyone, including myself, that we'll be back, in some way or another" (Sharma 2022). The litigants collectively decided not to seek leave to appeal to the High Court but vowed in a statement issued by their lawyers on 12 April

2022, to "continue direct action with hundreds of thousands of people around Australia pushing for climate action."[31]

The courage to express anger and speak truth to power – whether it be Brittany Higgins, Grace Tame, Kate, journalists, independents or young climate activists – is the same courage demonstrated by Second Wave feminists some 50 years ago. When truth is told, there is always a cost to the individual truth-teller exacted by patriarchy, but the courage that inspires women and girls to keep truth alive in every generation is a cause for celebration.

In the next chapter, I will discuss just how prevalent lying has become in the political arena, and issue a warning about the damage being done to democracy by leaders who treat truth as an optional extra.

---

[31] <https://equitygenerationlawyers.com/wp/wp-content/uploads/2022/04/220412-Statement-from-Sharma-litigants-on-High-Court-appeal.pdf>.

CHAPTER THREE

Lies, Damned Lies and the Death of Democracy

The contrast between the truth-telling of courageous women and men (as discussed in the previous chapter) and the lies and disinformation coming from the mouths of political leaders and many in the community today is stark.

An urgent question being asked by feminists and other social justice activists is: Will democracy survive the relentless attack on truth we are witnessing today? If, as historians of democracy insist, one of the imperatives for a healthy democracy is mutual understanding and trust, then the future is uncertain. In an interview with Jeffrey Goldberg in November 2020, Barack Obama commented:

> If we do not have the capacity to distinguish what's true from what's false, then by definition the marketplace of ideas doesn't work. We are entering into an epistemological crisis.[32]

While democracy encourages robust discussion on differing ideas, there must first be a willingness to hear each other and an ability to trust each other's word, and those are the ingredients that are seemingly in short supply in these early decades of the

---

32 Jeffrey Goldberg, 16 November 2020, 'Why Obama Fears for Our Democracy', *The Atlantic*. <https://www.theatlantic.com/ideas/archive/2020/11/why-obama-fears-for-our-democracy/617087/>.

twenty-first century. There has developed an extreme 'tribalism' that sees people on the left and the right closing their ears and their minds to all views except those of their own 'tribe'. Also, the blatant lies told by politicians in pursuit of power are leaving people confused and, consequently, trust is undermined.

In the current climate, many observers share Obama's concern that democracy itself may not survive, expressed variously as "the death of democracy" (Hett 2018); "democracy on the brink" (Schmidt 2020); "democracy lost" (Keane 2021); "existential threat to democracy" (Tiernan 2021); "democracy close to cardiac arrest" (Bowden and Teague 2022).

Characteristics of a democracy

Before looking at what some have expressed as threats to democracy, it will be helpful here to expand on the ideals and principles of democracy discussed in the Introduction, by setting out some of democracy's most commonly known characteristics.

Free and fair elections

Every adult has the right to vote for the candidate of their choice, to represent them in parliament for the term of the next government. Polling booths must be made accessible to those living in remote areas, as well as those in cities and towns, to ensure that all citizens are provided with equal opportunity to vote. [In Australia, voting is compulsory.]

Power belongs to all adult citizens through their freely elected representatives

The first duty of politicians is to ascertain the views of the people in their electorate and faithfully represent the views of the majority. Their loyalty must be to the people they represent rather than to the hierarchy of their own political party.

Majority rules

Under the Westminster system, the votes of the people are counted on election night under strict scrutiny, and the party that wins the majority of seats is invited by the Monarch or Governor-General to form government. There will be a peaceful transition of power and the new Prime Minister is required to govern in a non-partisan way – for *all* the people.

Individual rights and responsibilities

The civil liberties of individuals are protected, including freedom of speech and expression, the right to vote, the right to protest, and the right to protection under the law. Individual rights, however, will never extinguish one's responsibilities to other citizens. The free speech rights of one individual, for example, must never be used to deprive others of their right to speak and be heard. Rights are always balanced by responsibilities.

Freedom of the press

An independent media operates as a safeguard to the possible excesses of any government and, in granting licences to operate, government is required to ensure that no media company has a monopoly.

Independent judiciary and acceptance of the rule of law

An independent judiciary is another safeguard to the possible excesses of any government. While there is room for bias in the appointment of judges and magistrates by the government of the day, the appeal process in place in Australia and other places is intended to alleviate any bias that may occur.

Threats to democracy

One of the strengths of democracy as a form of government is that citizens, business leaders and politicians are all free to express their opinions and have them heard and considered by others. It is when trust in and respect for others breaks down that communities become hopelessly divided and democratic decision-making becomes impossible. Many today fear that major democratic countries including the United States, the United Kingdom and Australia, are fast approaching that point.

A chilling reminder of what can happen when a society descends into mob rule is presented by Benjamin Carter Hett in *The Death of Democracy: Hitler's Rise to Power and the Downfall of the Weimar Republic* (2018). Following Germany's downfall in World War I,

> ... the Weimar Republic created a state-of-the-art modern democracy with a scrupulously just proportional electoral system and protection for individual rights and freedoms, expressly including the equality of men and women. Germany had the world's most prominent gay rights movement ... an active feminist movement ... campaigns against the death penalty ... workers had won the eight-hour day with full pay (Hett 2018, pp. 6–7).

And yet, Hett continues, "out of this enlightened, creative, ultramodern democracy, grew the most evil regime in human history" (pp. 7–8).

How did this happen? Gripped by a growing contempt for the system, German society had become bitterly divided. A large number of political parties sprang up, each competing for power and the spoils of power. There was no attempt to find common ground, no interest in compromise, just a determination to win at any cost. Hett wrote:

CHAPTER THREE: LIES, DAMNED LIES AND THE DEATH OF DEMOCRACY

> For a democracy to work, all parties have to acknowledge that they have at least some minimal common ground and that compromises are both possible and necessary. By the 1930s, however, there was very little of this spirit left as German society grew ever more bitterly divided (pp. 13–14).

The climate was ripe for a decisive leader to rise up and take control and, when Adolf Hitler filled the void, the result was a total loss of democratic rights, World War II, and genocide on an unimaginable scale.

◈◈◈

Many today are seriously concerned that democracies are showing similar signs to those that resulted in the collapse of democracy in Germany: tribalism, abuse of democratic principles, ingrained inequality, political extremism, and the use of blatant lies and disinformation.

Tribalism

This is the term currently used to describe the deep divisions between groups of people that make any hope of democratic unity impossible. The divisions are much more complicated than the old left/right divide, with more and more groups demanding to be heard while, at the same time, closing their minds to the concerns of others. Social media enables people with similar complaints about the system to find each other, but also provides a platform from which to insult, threaten and vilify those with different views. Some issues attract strange bedfellows, for example, the Christian right supporting Donald Trump, or white supremacists and conspiracy theorists joining anti-vaccination protests. It is often a matter of 'the enemy of my enemy is my friend'. The system is the enemy. Some label those who advocate the need for scientific proof and rational thought 'elitist', while others label those who promote theories *without* scientific proof or rational thought 'deplorables'. The divisions extend also to the media. The particular arm of the media that reports and comments on the news in line with one's own theories is welcomed, while media that contradicts one's theories is pilloried as 'fake'.

Of great concern in terms of keeping democracy alive is the refusal to listen to others' opinions, lack of respect, hatred and complete resistance to any consideration of the need to compromise.

James Mumford, in *Vexed: Ethics Beyond Political Tribes* (2020), writes about the extreme polarisation evident today (Mumford 2020). Everyone today, he says, is put to a "political purity test" by members of one tribe or another and those who fail the test are ignored or ridiculed or threatened. In an interview with the ABC in Australia, Mumford stressed the need for basic democratic principles to be reinstated and an understanding that no one has a monopoly on the good. Because "there are competing visions of the good," he said, we need to try to build bridges instead of tearing one another down. Agreeing to disagree "does not mean we acquiesce." If we accept that there can be competing visions of the good, then we hold on to our own ethical position, while at the same time allowing that the other person may have a point.[33]

Abuse of democratic principles

The destructive forces of tribalism can also be found among politicians and political parties when, in their overwhelming need for power, they refuse to acknowledge any common ground with members of another party or the need to compromise for

---

33 Andrew West, 8 July 2020, 'Ethics Beyond Political Tribes', *ABC Radio National*. <https://www.abc.net.au/listen/programs/religionandethicsreport/vexed-ethics-beyond-political-tribes/12434756>.

CHAPTER THREE: LIES, DAMNED LIES AND THE DEATH OF DEMOCRACY

the good of the community. In their pursuit of power, there is clear evidence of abuse of democratic principles. Interference with free and fair elections is one of them.

During and since the presidency of Donald Trump in the United States, principles around free and fair elections, the right of every adult citizen to vote and the peaceful transition of power from one President to the next have all been under attack, particularly from the Republican side. Liz Cheney, Republican member of the House committee investigating the 6 January 2020 attack on the Capitol, placed the blame totally on her own party. "Our party has to choose," she said. "We can either be loyal to Donald Trump or we can be loyal to the constitution, but we cannot be both." Speaking of the need for people to understand how important their vote is, she reiterated: "We've got to be grounded on the rule of law … We've got to be grounded on fidelity of the constitution."[34] In some states, however, Republicans worked to enact laws designed to make voting more difficult for certain cohorts of citizens in an attempt to ensure that future elections favour Republican candidates. As reported in *The Guardian*:

> An avalanche of voter suppression laws is being pushed through in Republican-led states, from Arizona to Florida to Georgia to New Hampshire. Gerrymandered maps are being drawn up to form districts where demographics favour Republican candidates.
>
> Backers of Trump's big lie of a stolen election are running to be the secretary of state in many places, a position from which they would serve as the chief election official in their

---

34 Martin Pengelly, 3 January 2022, 'Capitol Attack: Cheney says Republicans Must Choose Between Trump and Truth', *The Guardian*. <https://theguardian.com/us-news/2022/jan/02/capitol-attack-liz-cheney-republicans-choose-trump-or-truth?CMP=Share_iOSApp_Other>.

state. Trump has endorsed such candidates in Michigan, Arizona, Georgia and Nevada – all crucial swing states.[35]

While some in the Republican Party accepted such tampering with the electoral system, the mid-term elections (2022), in which many of the candidates endorsed by Donald Trump failed in their bid to be elected, showed that the majority of voters still favoured free and fair elections.

However, the Democratic Party's attempt earlier that year to enact federal legislation to change the filibuster rules and establish federal rules enabling access to voting in all 50 states was voted down by Republicans with the help of two Democratic Party senators. The action of the two Democrats, said journalist Moira Donegan, "is now helping the Republican party to usher in an era of nationwide voter suppression and election subversion that will end meaningful representative government as we know it."[36]

Australian politics under Prime Minister Scott Morrison was also guilty of the abuse of democratic principles, though compulsory voting meant that deliberate suppression of voting was not usually one of them. The main issues under the Morrison and previous conservative governments were arguably the close relationship with generous party donors, the politicising of the public service (which, in fact, amounted to the hollowing out of the public service, one of the crucial elements of a fully functioning democracy), the expectation that elected politicians put the mandates of the party above the wishes and needs of the

---

35 <https://www.theguardian.com/us-news/2021/dec/19/republicans-subvert-democracy-democrats-paying-attention?CMP=Share_iOSApp_Other>.
36 Moira Donegan, 21 January 2022, 'Republican Voter Repression Is Rampant. Manchin and Sinema Are Complicit Now', *The Guardian*. <https://www.theguardian.com/commentisfree/2022/jan/20/republican-voter-suppression-is-rampant-manchin-and-sinema-are-complicit-now?CMP=Share_iOSApp_Other>.

CHAPTER THREE: LIES, DAMNED LIES AND THE DEATH OF DEMOCRACY

people they claimed to represent, and the use of public money for party political gain. Also, there was an obvious contempt for scrutiny and accountability.

Writing for the online newspaper *Crikey*, Bernard Keane penned a series of articles on the state of democracy in Australia during the years that Prime Minister Morrison's party was in power. One of the concerns he highlighted was the abuse of democratic principles. "Key democratic institutions in Australia are under attack at all levels," he wrote. He then listed: the Prime Minister's refusal "to establish a meaningful federal anti-corruption body"; the flouting of Freedom of Information laws; the stacking of the Administrative Appeals Tribunal "with scores of former Coalition MPs, staffers and allies"; and the politicising of the public service "with a long-term Liberal *apparatchik* now in charge of the public service" (Keane 2021).

Anne Tiernan, Professor of Politics and Dean of Engagement for the Griffith Business School, Griffith University in Brisbane, highlighted the "flagrant abuses revealed about the Morrison government's desperate efforts [in the 2019 election] to hold power." Writing in the same vein as Keane, she demonstrated what she called "an existential threat to Australian democracy" by the Morrison government:

> It remains unrestrained by its never-delivered commitment to establish a Federal Integrity Commission and emboldened by the lack of consequences for what, by any measure, is an egregious record by Commonwealth standards. [The threat is that] its disdain for scrutiny and accountability will become normalised as the way politics is done. And that like other once great democracies, Australia could sleepwalk towards authoritarian populism as key institutions are cynically attacked and undermined (Tiernan 2021).

Tiernan continues with a long list of abuses which reveal a total disregard for democratic traditions and conventions, including:

defiance of the Speaker of the House; "rorting and misuse of public funds"; "a penchant for secrecy and brazen refusal to answer questions"; lack of "accountability to parliament or in the media"; "failure to enforce the Ministerial or other Codes of Conduct"; and "abuses of power with respect to public appointments, the independence of public sector agencies, statutory bodies and the like."

Concerned about the state of democracy in Australia, the Australian Democracy Network conducted a series of interviews asking people what they perceived to be the key problems with Australia's democracy, and every person interviewed nominated "state capture" (sometimes calling it corporate capture or undue corporate influence) as the most serious problem. The Network's website describes it as "a problem eating away at the foundations of our democracy, our way of life and everything we care about most" (p. 5)[37] and offers this definition:

> State capture occurs when powerful or wealthy interests interfere with decision-making and assume a degree of control over the democratic rule-making process itself.[38]

It is particularly dangerous because "society's rule-making machinery is the prize, including the ability to define what constitutes corrupt or illicit behaviour in the first place" (p. 10).[39] This points directly to the concerns raised by Bernard Keane and Anne Tiernan that the government under Prime Minister Scott Morrison delayed appointing a Federal Integrity Commission because of its "disdain for scrutiny and accountability." The central task of such an Integrity Commission would be to call out

---

[37] <https://static1.squarespace.com/static/5eaac47ff5cd00162f5d23c1/t/621d5cc84fc34437e0d1df91/1646091511949/state+capture+report+2022+-+online.pdf>.

[38] Australian Democracy Network. February 2022. 'Confronting State Capture'. <https://australiandemocracy.org.au/statecapture>.

[39] <https://static1.squarespace.com/static/5eaac47ff5cd00162f5d23c1/t/621d5cc84fc34437e0d1df91/1646091511949/state+capture+report+2022+-+online.pdf>.

abuses of democratic principles. When the Morrison government lost the election in May 2022, it was clear that, among other things, voters were tired of waiting for the establishment of a meaningful Federal Integrity Commission. They had waited years for the Morrison government to fulfil its commitment to establishing one but had lost faith that it would ever eventuate. Before the election, the Labor Party promised to give priority to the setting up of a National Integrity Commission and, once elected, the current government under Prime Minister Anthony Albanese moved quickly to fulfil that promise.

Ingrained inequality

Where there is such outright abuse of democratic principles by politicians, it is not surprising to find serious inequality, since implementing the democratic principle of 'equal rights for all' would not be high on their agenda. In Australia, the working poor grow poorer as the cost of living increases and wages remain stagnant. So-called trickle-down economics favoured by conservative politicians sees governments giving tax breaks and other financial incentives to big and small businesses, while workers wait for a trickle-down benefit that never comes. The unemployed, also, suffer extreme poverty as successive governments stubbornly refuse to increase the unemployment benefit.

When governments show little or no interest in alleviating the pain and hopelessness of the economically disadvantaged, there often develops a blame mentality among those who struggle to get ahead. False theories can take hold, for example, "Indigenous people are always getting handouts from government," or "Refugees and immigrants are taking our jobs." From such false theories, racist attitudes multiply.

Inequality on the basis of race is fuelled by the attitudes of politicians as well as of ordinary citizens. In 2018, Senator

Fraser Anning called for "the final solution to the immigration problem" and Senator Pauline Hanson, a few months later, called on senators to endorse a motion (based on a white supremacist slogan) "it is OK to be white." As if that wasn't enough, Pauline Hanson deliberately drew attention to herself on the first sitting day of the new Parliament in 2022 by walking out of Parliament during the ceremonial Acknowledgement of Country by Indigenous Australians, shouting, "No I won't, and never will." Later in a statement, she declared that the Acknowledgement of Country "perpetuates racial division in Australia." On the One Nation Party's website, the explanation continued: "Senator Hanson considers this country belongs to her as much as it does belong to any other Australian, indigenous or otherwise."[40]

Writing in 2019, Tim Soutphommasane, Australia's Race Discrimination Commissioner from 2013 to 2018, called racism "a particular form of hatred" (p. 11), and warned that such hatred threatens to destroy democracy:

> Hate – specifically racial hatred – is threatening to become the new normal. If it does, it will destroy the very conditions for liberal democracy (Soutphommasane 2019, p. 17).

Echoing these words, Senator Penny Wong, in a speech accepting the McKinnon Prize in political leadership at the University of Melbourne in March 2019, focused on the threat to democracy inherent in racism and hate speech:

> There is a stark truth to which we must hold, racism is a threat to our democracy. Racism is not only unethical, it is antithetical to the values which underpin democracy. As Tim Soutphommasane reminds us, racism erodes the

---

[40] Molly Magennis, 27 July 2022, '"Extremely Disappointing": First Aboriginal Australian to Become Indigenous Minister Ken Wyatt Slams Pauline Hanson', *7News.com.au*. <https://7news.com.au/politics/pauline-hanson-storms-out-of-senate-during-acknowledgment-of-country-saying-it-perpetuates-racial-division-c-7658837>.

values of equality and justice and non-discrimination which are fundamental to liberal democracies. That is why our rejection of racism, of prejudice, of discrimination and of hate speech must be uncompromising (Wong 2019).

Political extremism

When governments fail to speak out against inequality, racism and hate speech, and act urgently to stamp them out, the way is left open for political extremism to flourish.

President Donald Trump's refusal to blame extremists for their violent and murderous behaviour is well known. Following the fatal Unite the Right rally in Charlottesville, Virginia, in August 2017, when the United States needed the kind of leadership from their president that would point the finger at political extremists with a view to stamping out hate and violence, he refused to condemn their actions. The people were left rudderless, and political extremism continued to flourish.

In March 2019, when an Australian white supremacist planned and carried out the murder of 51 Muslims in Christchurch, New Zealand (the victims were mostly men at prayer in two separate Mosques), one would have expected that the Australian government would respond urgently with condemnation of the kind of racism and hatred that white supremacist attitudes represent. There was acknowledgement of the pain New Zealanders were experiencing and sympathy for the terrible loss, but no determination to stamp out the ideas and attitudes that placed an Australian man on such a destructive and hate-filled path.

Writing in 2021 about the Australian situation, journalist Bernard Keane expressed alarm at the increase in extremist sentiment and activism:

> Extremism is increasing significantly, with security agencies warning that right-wing extremism is now a major threat,

white supremacist and US-imitating conspiracy theorists exploiting discontent over pandemic restrictions, and major party politicians urging civil disobedience and promoting anti-vaccine material (Keane 2021).

As Keane observed, Covid-19 restrictions saw the emergence of political extremism of the kind that had thousands of people demonstrating against mask-wearing and social distancing requirements. Encouraged by a few prominent politicians demanding 'freedom', protestors claimed that their freedoms were being taken away. Living in a democracy, they said, gave them the right to freedom of speech and expression at all times. Such extremism is a clear example of citizens demanding their own individual freedoms without reference to their responsibility to work together with others to keep the community as safe as possible during a deadly pandemic.

Lies and disinformation

The most serious worry of all in terms of the survival of democracy around the world is the evidence of lies and disinformation used mainly by politicians and their supporters, in the pursuit of power. A clear and rather spectacular example of the assault on truth is that perpetrated by the 45th President of the United States, Donald Trump, in his insistence that he won the 2020 US election in the face of solid evidence that he did not.

The evidence was clear. President Trump was soundly defeated by the 46th President, Joe Biden, who obtained upwards of 7 million more votes.[41] All except one of the legal challenges mounted by Donald Trump's team against the vote-counts in

---

41 There were 81,282,903 votes cast for Joe Biden and 74,223,030 votes cast for Donald Trump.

state after state failed.[42] His attempts at bullying and threatening Vice-President Mike Pence and other members of his own party to side with him and overturn the results of the election have come to nought. His alleged incitement of thousands of his supporters to march on the Capitol and stop the vote in Congress confirming Joe Biden as the 46th President, ended in six deaths, hundreds of arrests and a second impeachment, making Donald Trump the only president in US history to have been impeached twice. And yet, still he persists with the lie, and millions of Americans continue to support him.

In the lead-up to the 2024 presidential elections, Donald Trump led other Republican candidates by a wide margin even though there were four active indictments against him: 1) Business fraud charges, relating to the cover-up of $130,000 paid to adult film star Stormy Daniels; 2) Hoarding of classified documents at Mar-a-Lago in Florida; 3) Election interference (federally), charged with participating in a scheme to interfere with the peaceful transfer of power following the 2020 election of President Joe Biden; and 4) Election interference (Georgia), charged with trying to influence officials in that State to alter the vote count.[43]

With the Republican Party's support for Donald Trump and the support of millions of Americans holding strong, it is as if truth is relative, with no relationship to facts or proof or scientific evidence. Truth, it seems, can be whatever any individual person says it is. Indeed, with the *Washington Post* fact checker recording

---

42 Of around 50 lawsuits, all except one have been lost or withdrawn. <https://www.forbes.com/sites/alisondurkee/2020/12/08/trump-and-the-gop-have-now-lost-50-post-election-lawsuits/>.

43 <https://www.cbsnews.com/news/trump-indictments-details-guide-charges-trial-dates-people-case/>.

30,573 false or misleading claims by President Trump as of 20 January 2021,[44] truth appeared to be whatever he made up.

In the United Kingdom, too, there was serious concern about the ease with which Prime Minister Boris Johnson and his government lied to cover up mistakes, regardless of the diminishing effect such false representation has on democracy. Peter Osborne, award-winning writer and journalist, has kept a file on prime ministers' lies since the publication of his 2004 book *The Rise of Political Lying* in which he focused on the lies of British Prime Ministers John Major and Tony Blair. In his latest book, *The Assault on Truth: Boris Johnson, Donald Trump and the Emergence of a New Moral Barbarism* (2021), he argues that "the ruthless use of political deceit under the Johnson government is part of a wider attack on civilised values and traditional institutions across the Western world".[45] In addition to his writing, he set up a website to record the lies of Prime Minister Boris Johnson and his government.[46]

Osborne stresses that political lying has consequences:

Governments which get away with lies get away with the misgovernment the lies protect. They never take responsibility for error and failure. Billions of pounds are siphoned by cronies or simply wasted.

Service people give their lives in wrongful wars and there are thousands of premature avoidable deaths, not only

---

44 *The Washington Post*, 20 January 2021 (updated), 'In Four Years, President Trump Made 30,573 False or Misleading Claims'. <https://www.washingtonpost.com/graphics/politics/trump-claims-database/>.

45 Peter Osborne, 2021, *The Assault on Truth: Boris Johnson, Donald Trump and the Emergence of a New Moral Barbarism,* London: Simon and Schuster. <https://www.simonandschuster.co.uk/books/The-Assault-on-Truth/Peter-Oborne/9781398501003>.

46 Osborne, Peter and James Willcocks. 2024. 'Lies, Falsehoods and Misrepresentations from Boris Johnson to Keir Starmer'. *Political Lies*. <https://political-lies.co.uk/>.

CHAPTER THREE: LIES, DAMNED LIES AND THE DEATH OF DEMOCRACY

in pandemics, but in the normal course of bad government decisions on healthcare.

People lose trust in their governments and ignore them even when they are telling the truth. They therefore persist in behaviours which are harmful to them, their families, their community, their country and their planet.[47]

A similar situation occurred in Australia. Independent news outlet *Crikey* published a dossier of 48 "lies and falsehoods" of Prime Minister Scott Morrison from 21 December 2018 to 17 January 2022.[48] The editor of *Crikey* explained their motivation:

> We're doing this because we care deeply about our democracy and, like all Australians, we don't want to live in a country where systemic lying by our elected leader has become so normalised that no one seems to notice.[49]

Lucy Hamilton of the Australian Independent Media Network described the situation as she saw it:

> In Canberra at the moment there is an almost total lack of accountability. Any effort to confront Prime Minister Scott Morrison or his cabinet with their lies, corruption and ineptitude is met with deflection to a disingenuous list of 'achievements' or more lies (Hamilton 2022).

The telling of lies and half-truths in politics has become so commonplace that citizens seem to expect it and explain it away as something that politicians need to do in order to win elections. However, the damage such practices do to democracy itself is incalculable. For democracy to survive, a commitment to

---

47 Bridget Osborne, 29 November 2021, 'Peter Osborne lists Boris Johnson's Lies in New Website', *The Cheswick Calendar*. <https://chiswickcalendar.co.uk/peter-oborne-lists-boris-johnsons-lies-in-new-website/>.
48 Bernard Keane, Georgia Wilkins and David Hardaker, 25 May, 2021, 'A dossier of lies and falsehoods: How Scott Morrison manipulates the truth', *Crikey*. <https://www.crikey.com.au/dossier-of-lies-and-falsehoods/>.
49 Peter Fray and Eric Beecher, 25 May 2021, '"Without Truth, No Democracy Can Stand": Why We Are Calling Out the Prime Minister'. <https://www.crikey.com.au/2021/05/25/why-are-we-doing-this-scott-morrison/>.

truth-telling is imperative. Simon Longstaff, executive director of The Ethics Centre in Sydney, pleads with citizens not to forget "how important the truth is to a functioning democracy." He continues:

> [W]ithout truth no democracy can stand. This is because without truth there can be no informed consent, because without truth there can be no informed citizens.
>
> Misleading citizens (even unintentionally) is a body-blow to democracy because all authority ultimately flows from those who have been misled …
>
> To deny access to the truth is to imperil the legitimacy of the democratic system as a whole because, in the end, it risks being built on nothing true.[50]

In the Philippines, too, the situation is dire. During the presidency of Rodrigo Duterte (2016–2022), opponents were falsely accused, arrested and, in some cases, will spend years in prison. When Senator Leila de Lima called for investigations into the extrajudicial killings ordered by Duterte early in his Presidency, she was charged with running a drug trafficking ring and was incarcerated in prison for more than six years awaiting trial on trumped up charges of taking bribes from drug lords. It was feared that Senator de Lima, who was Justice Secretary in a previous government and chair of the Human Rights Commission, could be jailed for life. The Speaker of the House of Representatives called her "the number one drug lord in the whole Philippines." During her imprisonment, her supporters kept count of the number of days that she was detained:

> A human rights defender and social justice champion, Sen. Leila M. de Lima remains unjustly detained to this day (2645 days and counting) for speaking truth to power.[51]

---

50 Simon Longstaff, 25 May 2021, 'The truth is precious. Let's not take it for granted', *Crikey*. <https://crikey.com.au/2021/05/25/truth-is-precious/>.
51 Leila de Lima. <https://leiladelima.ph>.

CHAPTER THREE: LIES, DAMNED LIES AND THE DEATH OF DEMOCRACY

The counting stopped following the 2023 elections when Ferdinand Marcos Jr replaced Rodrigo Duterte as president and former Senator de Lima was released on bail. Already, five witnesses against her have recanted their testimonies, making it very likely that she will soon be acquitted of all charges. It is expected by her supporters that she will put her energy into campaigning for a case against Duterte at the International Criminal Court (Cabato 2023).

Another courageous woman in the Philippines is journalist Maria Ressa, who heads up the news site *Rappler*. She and her team produced research revealing the way social networks were coordinated and deployed to boost support for Duterte in the 2016 presidential elections. Speaking with a journalist from CBC news, she said:

> Democracy as we know it is dead. What you're seeing is exponential growth of propaganda networks that hijack what used to be called democracy.

Then, commenting on the campaign to silence anyone who spoke out in opposition to Duterte, she continued:

> You look at anyone who says anything against the killings, against the drug war, especially if they are women, they will get clobbered on social media. They are threatened with death, with rape. You name it, it's happened.[52]

Maria Ressa was arrested and, in June 2020, the BBC reported that she had been found guilty of libel:

> The former CNN journalist is the head of a news site that's critical of strongman President Rodrigo Duterte. A writer for the site, Rappler, was also convicted. Both have been released on bail pending appeal – but could face six years in prison. Ressa denied the charges and claimed they were politically

---

52 CBC News, 27 April 2017, '"Democracy As We Know It Is Dead": Filipino Journalists Fight Fake News'. <https://www.cbc.ca/news/world/democracy-as-we-know-it-is-dead-filipino-journalists-fight-fake-news-1.4086920>.

motivated. But the president and his supporters have accused her, and her site, of reporting fake news.[53]

In September 2023, Ressa was acquitted of tax evasion charges that the Duterte government had brought against her and the *Rappler* site. The appeal against the guilty verdict for charges of cyber-libel brought against her and former colleague Rey Santos Jr, however, is still pending.[54]

In contrast to the principled stance taken by Senator de Lima and Maria Ressa, Davao City Mayor Sara Duterte, daughter of President Rodrigo Duterte, said during the 2019 senatorial elections that voters "should not be making an issue out of honesty" because all politicians trade in untruths (*Philippine Daily Inquirer* 2021).

Once again, in the 2022 election in the Philippines, social media was used to spread false information, resulting in the election of Ferdinand Marcos Jr as President and Sara Duterte as Vice President.[55]

How has it come to this?

How can it be that, regardless of the existential threat to democracy caused by such trading in untruths, many politicians still choose lies and deceit over truth and integrity? Is neoliberalism to blame? Has neoliberalism caused a 'win at any cost' mentality? Maybe postmodernism is to blame. Has postmodernism with its insistence on fluidity had such an influence that nothing of any substance matters – even truth? Or is it liberalism? Has liberalism

---

53 <https://www.bbc.com/news/world-asia-53046052>.
54 <https://www.aljazeera.com/news/2023/9/12/nobel-laureate-maria-ressa-acquitted-in-philippines-tax-evasion-case>.
55 22 July 2022, 'Highlights: Rappler+Briefing on the Social Media Landscape in the 2022, Philippine Elections', *Rappler.com*. <https://www.rappler.com/nation/elections/highlights-plus-briefing-social-media-landscape-2022-elections/>.

encouraged such an arrogant individualism that shared values and common decency count for nothing any more? Or is it the growing adherence to libertarianism evident today? A brief look at each of these will, I suggest, reveal that they have all been involved to some extent in the putting aside of truth in favour of the pursuit of power and personal advancement.

Neoliberalism

Neoliberalism is the term used by many to denote an economic philosophy associated with free-market capitalism. It seeks to increase the role of the market and influence governments to prioritise free trade agreements, privatisation, deregulation and austerity measures. Noam Chomsky and Marv Waterstone's description of the central tenets of neoliberalism is helpful:

> The central tenets include the elimination (or preferably the privatization) of government services of all kinds, an all-out assault on the ability of labor to organize, the massive deregulation of every segment of the economy, and the absolute faith in market-based principles to adjudicate all elements of social, political, cultural, and economic life (Chomsky and Waterstone 2021, p. x).

Susan Hawthorne, in *Vortex: The Crisis of Patriarchy*, adds an important dimension to any discussion of neoliberalism. She paints a picture of a vortex "getting ever deeper, swirling ever faster and wider, evermore out of control":

> The vortex of patriarchy encompasses the deep deceptions of capitalism at its worst where entitlement, consumerism and celebrity culture are held up as cues for happiness, while the world's majority live in dire poverty and where the environment continues to be plundered (Hawthorne 2020, p. 1).

The United Kingdom under Prime Minister Margaret Thatcher, the United States under President Ronald Reagan and Australia under Prime Minister John Howard all adopted neoliberal economic policies, and ordinary citizens were the losers. The austerity measures introduced in each country saw an attack on unions, workers' wages stagnating with the cost of living continuing to increase, a lessening of the importance of welfare and a 'user-pays' mentality. Governments made it clear that there were to be no 'handouts'. At the same time, people saw governments giving generous tax breaks to businesses, CEOs receiving enormous, multi-million dollar salaries and a reinterpretation of the concept of human rights.

Jessica Whyte, in *The Morals of the Market: Human Rights and the Rise of Neoliberalism,* investigates "the historical and conceptual relations between human rights and neoliberalism," and concludes that neoliberalism used the concept of human rights in order to defend the rights of capital. She speaks of "the ease with which human rights discourses have been mobilised in defence of wealth and power in the period of neoliberal hegemony" (Whyte 2019, pp. 3–4). While rejecting the idea of equality and the need for welfare, she says, the free market nevertheless needed a moral foundation. In its reinterpretation of human rights, the focus moved from community responsibilities to individual freedom. There was a suspension of democracy and an emphasis on survival of the successful. Human rights required individual freedom and individual freedom required free market competition. In an unequal world, it is up to the disempowered individual to pull himself/herself up and become a player in the new economic climate.[56]

Drawing attention to "the crimes of neoliberal capitalist patriarchy," Susan Hawthorne agrees that the reinterpretation of

---

56   Andrew West, 29 January 2020, 'Human Rights, Neoliberalism and the Morals of the Market', *The Religion and Ethics Report*. <https://www.abc.net.au/radio national/programs/religionandethicsreport/january-29-2020/11909880>.

CHAPTER THREE: LIES, DAMNED LIES AND THE DEATH OF DEMOCRACY

human rights to focus on individual freedom actually denies the majority of people their basic rights. As she puts it:

> The vortex is particularly destructive of those who are caught up in its empty centre, as are people with disabilities, Indigenous and poverty stricken peoples, the landless and refugees. Among all these groups are women who bear an unreasonable load of poverty and violence against them.

It is "capitalism without compassion or conscience," she adds (Hawthorne 2020, pp. 1–2).

One can only conclude that neoliberalism, and its promise of a better life for all, is based on a lie. The truth is that equal economic and social participation is not possible in a ruthless, competitive market, when the life circumstances of the individuals involved are very different.

The woman who lives in fear of her violent partner, for example, has no freedom to enjoy the fruits of the free market. "Why doesn't she leave him?" ask the uninformed. The reason lies in the fact that he has threatened many times that, if she ever tried to leave him, he would kill her and the children. She is aware, of course, of the statistics revealing that some violent men do indeed kill their partners and/or children following their bid for freedom. She has read with horror the story of Hannah Clarke and her three children, six-year-old Aaliyah, four-year-old Laianah, and three-year-old Trey, who were incinerated in their car when their estranged husband and father threw petrol in and around the car and set it alight.[57] She has read, too, the story of the father who threw his four-year-old daughter off a

---

57   Blake Antrobus, 7 December 2021, '"Indescribable Horror": Inquest Told of Hannah Clarke's Final Words, Heroic Last Act Before Death', News.com.au <https://www.news.com.au/national/queensland/courts-law/indescribable-horror-coroner-to-probe-shocking-murder-of-hannah-clarke-and-three-kids/news-story/d41b006d6d1861a665cb8abccd4c32ea>.

bridge in Melbourne to her death.[58] Why not throw himself off the bridge and let his daughter live, one may ask? Because his aim was to inflict maximum pain on his ex-partner who had found the courage to separate from him.

Many women living with violent men choose to stay and endure the violence, abuse and insults, all the while trying to protect their children from the effects of the abuse they witness. Even though the children will be badly affected, the mothers reason, at least they will still be alive. What is the free market doing for these women and their children?

Also, how is the free market benefiting the Indigenous man who turned to alcohol to deaden the effects of the racial abuse he experienced in his school years right through to his attempts to find work in his adult years? Or the woman living with a disability who suffered sexual abuse throughout her childhood and financial abuse, in more recent times, by the worker employed to care for her?

And what is the free market doing to ensure the individual freedoms of refugees and asylum-seekers?[59]

The senseless cruelty of an Australian government could not be demonstrated more clearly than in relation to the young Tamil family who came to be known as the Biloela family. Nades

---

58 Ashlynne McGhee, 15 July 2015, 'Darcey Freeman Inquest: Doctors Knew Father Who Threw 4yo off Melbourne's West Gate Bridge Was Violent, Court Hears', *ABC News*. <https://www.abc.net.au/news/2015-07-15/doctors-knew-freeman-was-violent-before-bridge-murder/6620082.>.

59 The Australian Government began sending asylum-seekers who came by boat to processing centres on Nauru and Manus Island in 2001. The practice of offshore processing was discontinued in 2008 but started again in 2012. Many were kept in detention for ten years or more. While there are still around 80 refugees on Manus Island, the last of those kept on Nauru had been evacuated by June 2023 (Doherty and Gillespie 2023). The processing centre on Nauru, however, remains open at a cost of $350m a year to Australian taxpayers. When a boat arrived in September 2023, those asylum-seekers were sent to Nauru. Offshore processing and detention are still live options, it seems, for those seeking a better life in Australia (Karp 2023).

CHAPTER THREE: LIES, DAMNED LIES AND THE DEATH OF DEMOCRACY

and Priya Murugappan came to Australia separately, met and married in Sydney, and moved to the regional Queensland town of Biloela. Their two daughters, Kopika and Tharnicaa, were born in Biloela. Nades worked at the meatworks and Priya volunteered in several charities while caring for her young daughters. Without warning, the family were snatched from their home in Biloela at around 4 a.m. by officials in Prime Minister Scott Morrison's government and placed in detention in March 2018, because they did not have a visa to stay in the country. Soon they were transferred to the detention facility on Christmas Island where they remained for two years. Throughout that time, the citizens of Biloela called for the return of this Sri Lankan family who, they argued, had contributed much to their community. But the government seemed determined to ignore the groundswell of support and continued to refuse them valid visas. In June 2021, Tharnicaa became very ill and had to be flown with her mother to a hospital in Perth. After a few weeks, the government succumbed to pressure and released the family from detention on Christmas Island to live in Perth but still did not grant them freedom of movement. They had to continue to live in Perth, could not return to Biloela and remained under threat of being deported back to Sri Lanka. At the beginning of 2021, it was reported that the cost to Australian taxpayers of keeping this one family in detention had reached $6 million. One of the first things the Albanese Government did following its success in the May 2022 election was to grant this family permission to return to their home in Biloela. Then, on 5 August, they received permanent residency in Australia.[60]

I ask again: What did the free market do to alleviate the pain, distress and hopelessness this Biloela family experienced, and

---

[60] <https://www.sbs.com.au/news/article/from-sri-lanka-to-biloela-to-perth-and-back-a-timeline-of-the-nadesalingam-familys-journey/jfmofat70>.

what is the free market doing for women living in fear of their partner's violence, for victims of racial discrimination, for people with disabilities suffering from sexual and/or economic abuse, or for refugees and asylum-seekers? How are the 'human rights' of neoliberalism helping them?

Postmodernism

Another trend that has played a huge part in the current assault on truth is that of postmodernism – the social theory that considered itself more progressive than any previous theories and trashed wholesale and incorrectly everything about the modernist era.

Postmodernism criticises norms and values because, it says, they result from the ideology of elitist groups. Science and technology should not be trusted because they are said to be instruments of established power. There is no such thing as objective truth. Reason and logic are suspect. Nothing is certain. In other words, postmodern theory is characterised by scepticism, relativism and suspicion of reason.

Feminist critics of postmodernism accuse its proponents of nihilism (the theory of nothingness), emptiness and meaninglessness; and of obscurantism, the practice of presenting theories in a deliberately obscure way so as, some would say, to limit further discussion and understanding.

Postmodernism, with its emphasis on relativism and fluidity, has promoted the idea of post-truth. Truth is not to be relied on because civilisation has moved beyond the notion of objective truth, they say. Truth is fluid. When scientific evidence is not to be trusted, then truth is freed up to be whatever any individual says it is.

Kellyanne Conway, when she was adviser to President Donald Trump, famously used the phrase "alternative facts," implying that there may be facts, but there are also alternative facts. There was no longer any need, it seemed at the time, for truth to be a shared imperative. Such a proposition is alarming, not only because it implies that there are no absolute truths but, also, because it signals the disappearance of shared objective standards for truth. If there is to be any hope of harmony between nations as well as between individuals, an agreed understanding of truth is imperative.

Hannah Arendt warned against a "defactualised environment" in which factual truths are

> ... always in danger of being perforated by single lies or torn to shreds by the organised lying of groups, nations, or classes, or denied and distorted, often carefully covered up by reams of falsehoods ... (Arendt 1972, pp. 6–7).

Hannah Arendt's "defactualised environment" is a fair description of the post-truth mentality on display today from many politicians, political parties, business leaders and many in the community. In fact, lies, denials, distortions and spin have become so common that people have come to expect such falsehoods and seem to accept them as part of the political and social discourse. Such a situation is a tragedy.

Postmodernism's notion of fluidity is another area of great concern. Many feminists call it out as a convenient theory that seeks to erase women as a social class. Indeed, in an attempt to accommodate the demands of the trans lobby, governments, universities and many in the community (including some liberal feminists) insist that all language be gender-neutral, omitting any reference to sex. One politician who had the courage to hold out against the trans lobby was Bill Shorten, Government Services Minister in the Albanese Government. When he saw that the government's Medicare forms had been changed to reflect gender-neutral language, he ordered that 'birthing parent' be removed and replaced by 'mother'. Bill Shorten was immediately accused of being transphobic, anti-queer and 'out of touch'.

Among the objections, also, was the claim that many men are birthing parents (54 men in 2017, they claimed) and that they were being excluded by the minister's ruling. What the objectors failed to mention, however, was that 'men' were able to give birth only because they were actually biological women who still had the functioning women's bodies they were born with. 'Birthing parent' is one term among many that the powerful trans lobby is insisting on. 'Pregnant person' is another. Instead of breast milk, they insist on 'chest milk' or 'human milk'; instead of breast-feeding, they insist on 'chest-feeding', and on and on it goes.

A serious concern among some midwives and others in the community is that 'gender', the word we use to describe the *socially constructed* characteristics of those we define as men and women, is being promoted above 'sex', the word we use to describe the *biological and physiological* characteristics of males and females. Basic biological facts are being replaced by social constructs.

Another concern about postmodernism's concept of gender fluidity is that it conveniently wipes out men's ongoing oppression of women. In 1996, Diane Bell and Renate Klein edited a book, now a feminist classic, *Radically Speaking: Feminism Reclaimed*, in which they challenged postmodernism as a theory that rendered "women's ongoing multifaceted oppressions by men as … at best irrelevant, at worst non-existent" (Bell and Klein (Eds) 1996, p. xx).

When the binary, man/woman, is replaced by gender as non-binary, men's violence against women, rape of women, oppression of women become irrelevant or non-existent. In a postmodern world, sex-defining pronouns (he/she, his/hers) are seen as divisive and oppressive and there is a demand to replace them with 'they' and 'them'. To illustrate the lengths postmodernism has gone to erase the truth of men's violence against women, instead of saying 'he raped her', the requirement now is to say 'they raped them'. Feminists and other workers in women's services who confront the results of men's violence toward women every day, insist that the truth about misogyny and the violence that ensues must be exposed and the men who perpetrate such violence be held accountable.

The same is true of racism. When the requirement is to be non-discriminating in one's discussion about racism, the scene is set for the continuing dominance of those who are racist and the continuation of racist speech and behaviour. For a problem to be faced and dealt with, it must first be named. The truth about racism in Australia is that men and women of the dominant racial group (i.e. Caucasian) enjoy a power and privilege not extended to Indigenous or other ethnic minorities. For racism to be stamped out, it is imperative that perpetrators of racism, hate speech and violence be exposed and held accountable.

Postmodernism's attempt to erase misogyny and racism by the use of 'inclusive' language, thereby ensuring that justice is never brought to bear on perpetrators, creates an environment where truth and responsibility for one's actions is non-existent.

Liberalism

Liberalism is another system that must be interrogated in this quest to understand how lies and disinformation are so often chosen today over truth, and why such deceit is attempted with little or no obvious sense of shame.

The basic tenets of liberalism: individual freedom, fairness, respect for the dignity of others, generosity, reciprocity, are almost unrecognisable today as those who profess to value liberalism place their own individual freedom above all else. For them, the liberal value of individual freedom is used to justify behaviour that is unrestrained and excessive. In many, it has created a self-focus, a sense of privilege that results in feelings of dissatisfaction when life's rewards don't flow to them to the degree that they feel they deserve. Often there develops a resentment of the achievements of others that, in many cases, is used to justify abuse or trolling or exploitation.

The excesses of liberalism that are, in fact, excesses resulting from an extreme focus on the individual, will be examined in some detail in Chapter Five.

Libertarianism

Based on the liberal principle of 'individual freedom', libertarianism takes it a step further and states that, "liberty is the most important political value." Libertarians criticise governments who, they say, take on themselves wide-ranging powers to control people's lives instead of allowing individuals the freedom to live as they please. They are highly critical, too, of the systems democracy has in place for the purpose of maintaining order and harmony. Referring to government agencies and departments as 'agents of the state', they say:

> Legislators, bureaucrats, police, and other agents who enforce the state's commands treat other people as pawns on a chessboard to be maneuvered into whatever configuration they deem best. Too many fail to see people as independent agents with their own desires and plans.[61]

Many today who feel powerless to improve their economic and social status seem to be moving toward an extreme libertarian focus, freely expressing anti-democratic sentiments. They reject the legitimacy of governments, turn their backs on history and tradition, label science and education as elitist, criticise the media as 'fake' and, in so many ways, separate themselves from the democratic establishment. Movements like the sovereign

---

61 <https://www.libertarianism.org/what-is-a-libertarian>.

CHAPTER THREE: LIES, DAMNED LIES AND THE DEATH OF DEMOCRACY

citizen phenomenon are growing and its adherents becoming more vocal.[62]

At the political level, the Make America Great Again (MAGA) movement is based on libertarian principles. The aim of leaders like Steve Bannon (who was CEO of Donald Trump's 2016 presidential campaign and served as chief White House strategist for the first seven months of his presidency) is to destroy established political parties and democratic principles, and replace them with far-right MAGA movement rule.[63]

For now, I conclude this section by reiterating that both liberalism and libertarianism today are contaminated by a hyper-individualism and a pathological self-focus which sees many people blinded to the responsibilities of living in society with others. Lies and the spreading of disinformation are commonplace, shaking the foundations of democracy itself. For democracy to work, there needs to be a shared understanding of and respect for truth, an acceptance that the freedoms of liberalism are for all, and a commitment to ensuring that the freedoms of others are as protected as one's own.

In light of the fact that many democratic governments throughout the world have allowed themselves to be seriously influenced by the demands of neoliberalism, postmodernism and liberalism, it will be helpful here to pause and examine some of the tactics used in an effort to side-step the truth, using the Australian political situation as an example.

---

62   The sovereign citizen movement became apparent in the United States in the 1970s and has since expanded to other democratic countries including Canada and Australia. Members claim that they are not subject to the laws of the land, reject the need for drivers' licences and vehicle registration, and are prepared to fight for their sovereign citizen rights in court if and when the need arises.

63   <https://www.theguardian.com/us-news/2024/apr/04/steve-bannon-book-maga>.

CHAPTER FOUR

Creative Ways of Avoiding the Truth

In this age of postmodern confusion, some of the tactics commonly used by politicians and others intent on avoiding the truth can be quite creative. Here I am choosing to call the beliefs behind those tactics 'isms'. An 'ism' is a doctrine or a system of belief, and a study of social and political movements reveals that there are a multitude of 'isms' being used by governments and individual citizens to facilitate the setting aside of truth under the guise of offering 'respectable' and 'sincere' responses.

To illustrate this point, I will focus on five 'isms' that social justice activists will recognise as deliberate attempts by those in power to ensure that the status quo is undisturbed, and to frustrate the efforts of activists who seek to advocate on behalf of those whose power is diminished by discrimination and neglect. They are: gradualism, equalism, whataboutism, waititoutism and hideandseekism.

Gradualism

In social justice theory, gradualism refers to a policy of gradual reform as opposed to radical action. A convenient belief held by many in mainstream society is that change that occurs gradually is much more likely to last, but it is often the case that such gradualism only serves to preserve the status quo and entrench existing offences against human rights. The idea of gradual emancipation of slaves, for example, simply stimulated the trade. In the United States, any suggestion of the gradual cutting back of citizens' rights to own and carry guns, assault rifles and weapons of mass destruction usually prompts a huge increase in sales at gun shops. People rush to buy weapons to add to their arsenal while they are still available.

In political parties, too, a commitment to gradualism affects the representation of women and racial minorities. In order to increase the number of women in parliament, progressive political parties in Australia introduced quotas to good effect, but conservative parties insist that candidates should be selected on merit. As history shows, if a political party does not set a goal of achieving equality of the sexes by the use of quotas, the standards for merit continue to include 'being male'. Prime Minister Scott Morrison said in his International Women's Day speech in 2019:

> … we're not about setting Australians against each other, trying to push some down to lift others up. That's not in our values. That is an absolutely Liberal value, that you don't push some people down to lift some people up. And that is true about gender equality too. We want to see women rise. But we don't want to see women rise only on the basis of others doing worse.[64]

Echoing comments from women all around the country, Angela Priestly for *Women's Agenda* wrote. "Presumably, by others, he means at the expense of *men*" (Priestly 2019). No party has yet introduced quotas for racial minorities.

---

64 Belinda Jepsen, 8 March 2019, 'Scott Morrison Just Made the Worst International Women's Day Speech in the History of Forever', *Mamamia*. <https://www.mamamia.com.au/scott-morrison-international-womens-day/>.

CHAPTER FOUR: CREATIVE WAYS OF AVOIDING THE TRUTH

Gradualism is the theory also employed by some therapists working with people fighting addictions. The idea is that a person addicted to alcohol or drugs can reduce their use to five days a week, then to three days a week, till they reach a point where they feel their lives are no longer dominated by alcohol or drugs. Another gradual treatment with the alcohol-addicted is to limit oneself to ten drinks a day, then six, and so on. The respected organisation, Alcoholics Anonymous, is adamant that such gradualism only encourages an addicted person to continue drinking. Radical action in the form of total abstinence, with the availability of 24-hour support, is the only way to achieve an alcohol-free future, they insist.

Social justice activists speaking out against sexism, racism, classism, ableism and all other forms of discrimination against the disempowered, and insisting that governments address the serious inequalities that exist, reject gradualism as an unjustifiable compromise in situations where radical action is required.

Feminists all around the world are tired of hearing the words "not yet," "be patient," "change must happen slowly." Second Wave feminists called for revolution in the 1970s and 1980s and what they received was gradualism – painfully slow change. And every change, every gain, has only been achieved after a long hard fight by determined women. Still today, regardless of assurances coming from the mouths of politicians, it is clear to feminists that patriarchal leaders have no intention of sharing their power with women until forced to do so. Consequently, generation after generation of feminists have mounted incredibly strong campaigns to win rights for women: voting rights; property rights; equal opportunity in education and employment; laws against rape in marriage; rights over one's own body; the right to safety against men's violence in the home; laws against the sexual abuse of children; laws against sexual harassment in the workplace; and so on. Many of those campaigns are ongoing with no appreciable change to the status quo due, no doubt, to the fact that men and male-dominated institutions show little enthusiasm for laws developed to benefit women.

Climate change activists, too, continue to be frustrated by the slow pace of change. Gradualism has been the response of governments in the thrall of business leaders and multinational corporations even when the evidence is clear that action on climate change to save the planet from disaster is urgently needed. Until recently, the Australian Government has been slow to grasp the need for action. When Australia's former Prime Minister, Scott Morrison, was the nation's Treasurer in 2017, he took a lump of coal into the parliament and taunted the Labor opposition and the Greens because of their commitment to renewable energy, saying: "Don't be afraid, don't be scared, it won't hurt you. It's coal." Clive Hamilton, Professor of Public Ethics at the Centre for Applied Philosophy and Public Ethics (CAPPE) at Charles Sturt University, writing in *The Conversation*, reminded readers that this "… audacious celebration of the wonders of coal occurred in the middle of one of the most severe heatwaves eastern Australia ever experienced" (Hamilton 2017). The urgent need for climate action was treated as a joke in this 2017 theatrical performance in parliament by a government intent on pleasing its masters in the fossil fuel industry.

Australia's allies across the world were becoming more and more frustrated by Australia's flippant attitude to climate change under the Morrison Government, especially given the abundance of renewable energy Australia has access to all year round: sunlight, wind, hydro, wave. One would have thought that the repeated devastating bushfires,[65] the increasing intensity

---

65   Statista Research Department, 4 April 2024, 'Bushfires in Australia – Statistics and Facts', *Statista*. <https://www.statista.com/topics/6125/bushfires-in-australia/#topicHeader__wrapper>.

of cyclones, the unprecedented flooding events in different parts of Australia would have woken them up to the urgency of the situation. But conservative politicians persisted in their determination to 'achieve' a reduction in greenhouse gas emissions through gradualism, i.e., natural processes, rather than radical action. When Prime Minister Anthony Albanese's government came to power in 2022, it moved quickly to pass legislation setting a target of 43% greenhouse gas emissions reduction by 2030 and, while the Greens and other climate activists are still critical of the gradualism implicit in Labor's target when radical action is desperately needed, they accept that it is an important start.

How do governments usually implement gradualism? Under pressure from activists to right the wrongs done to vulnerable groups and to the planet, governments often employ a gradual response to give the impression that they do, indeed, care and are working toward change. Favourite responses include: setting up royal commissions; instigating a series of inquiries; and forming focus groups required to report back to government. *Crikey* journalist, Bernard Keane, described what he saw as the role of inquiries in the government of Prime Minister Scott Morrison:

> Inquiries are the accountability theatre of the Morrison government – carefully structured, ritualistic, almost kabuki-like set-pieces that always play out the same way at excruciating length, and in which literally nothing ever happens. Nothing is intended to happen – their goal is to prevent action, not enable it (Keane 2022).

To illustrate the lack of action that usually ensues from a commitment to gradualism, I have chosen three areas that have long been of concern to activists in Australia: aged care, Indigenous wellbeing and women's safety.

Aged care

Australia's response to the entrenched problems in the aged care sector is a classic example of the failure of gradualism. Since 1997, there have been two acts of parliament, 20 inquiries into the aged care system, several reviews and one royal commission and still, very little has changed. The following are some of the time-wasting, money-wasting responses employed as a way of avoiding rapid and radical action.

Acts of Parliament
1997: Commonwealth Aged Care Act
2013: Living Longer Living Better Act

Inquiries
2011: Caring for Older Australians
2015: Residential and Community Aged Care in Australia
2018: Quality of Care in Residential Aged Care Facilities in Australia
2020: Special Report on COVID-19 and Aged Care

Reviews
In response to the recommendations from these and other inquiries throughout the years, the Government set up various reviews:
- An Ageing Consultative Committee
- A National Aged Care Forum
- A Taskforce
- A Roundtable of key stakeholders
- A Quality in Community Care Reference group
- An Aged Care Workforce Committee

Also, the Australian Government developed a Charter of Aged Care Rights in 2019, to replace the 1997 Charter of Care Recipients' Rights and Responsibilities – Residential Care.

In September 2018, then Prime Minister Scott Morrison set up the Royal Commission into Aged Care Quality and Safety, the

CHAPTER FOUR: CREATIVE WAYS OF AVOIDING THE TRUTH

final report of which was tabled in Parliament in October 2020.[66] While the Commissioners pointed to what has been called "a shocking tale of neglect" in aged care, there remains scepticism among citizens that the recommendations will receive the urgent attention they deserve (Phillips, Parker and Woods 2018).

Clearly, what is needed to improve aged care substantially in Australia is not gradualism, but urgent radical action: a substantial rise in funding, an increase in remuneration from the pitifully low wages aged care workers currently receive, regulation stipulating ratio of nursing staff to residents and ongoing scrutiny by a regulator to ensure the standards of care, diet, cleanliness, etc., are of a consistently high quality.

Instead of continuing to avoid the truth about the seriousness of the aged care situation in Australia, such radical action could be implemented immediately.

Indigenous wellbeing

The wellbeing of Indigenous Australians is another area that points to the failure of gradualism as a theory to effect much-needed change. In 1967, Aboriginal and Torres Strait Islander people were finally granted the right to vote following a referendum in which more than 90% of Australians registered a YES vote, enabling a change in the constitution.

Since that time, there have been several major inquiries set up for the purpose of improving the situation for Indigenous Australians in the face of continuing discrimination and vilification but, as is the way with gradualism, very little change has been achieved.

1987: *Royal Commission into Aboriginal Deaths in Custody* – final report presented in 1991.

---

66   Royal Commission into Aged Care Quality and Safety, 2020. <https://www.health.gov.au/health-topics/aged-care/aged-care-reforms-and-reviews/royal-commission-into-aged-care-quality-and-safety>.

1987–1991: National Archives guide to *Aboriginal Deaths in Custody: The Royal Commission and its Records.*

1989–1996: Australian Human Rights Commission, Indigenous Deaths in Custody inquiry. *Indigenous Deaths in Custody.*

1997: Australian Human Rights Commission. *Bringing Them Home: Report of the National Inquiry into the Separation of Aboriginal and Torres Strait Islander Children from Their Families.*

2000: Senate Standing Committee. *HEALING: A Legacy of Generations* (Report on the Stolen Generations Inquiry).

2006: Senate Standing Committee. *Unfinished Business: Indigenous Stolen Wages.* (Report on the inquiry into stolen wages).

2011: House of Representatives Standing Committee. *Doing Time – Time for Doing: Indigenous Youth in the Criminal Justice System.*

In addition, there is the *National Agreement on Closing the Gap* established in 2008 to address Indigenous disadvantage. Under the agreement, federal, state and local governments work with Aboriginal and Torres Strait Islander peoples to bridge the gap between Indigenous and non-Indigenous citizens in several key areas: early childhood, education, health, economics, healthy homes, safe communities, governance and leadership. The ten-year report in 2018 showed that progress has been slow, with only three of the target areas close to meeting targets: halving the gap in child mortality by 2018; ensuring that 95% of all Indigenous four-year-olds are enrolled in early childhood education by 2025; and halving the gap in Year 12 attainment by 2020. Important areas such as health, life expectancy, employment, economics and community safety still had a long way to go.

The *Closing the Gap Report* of 2022 revealed similar disappointing results, with four of the target areas actually going backwards: children's school readiness, incarceration rates, suicide rates and child-removal rates.[67] On a positive note, the Albanese Government has produced the *2023 Commonwealth Closing the Gap Implementation Plan* and, in addition, has committed $424 million to be spent on clean water, food security, housing, and domestic and family violence-related issues in Indigenous communities.

The *Closing the Gap Report 2023* revealed that four target areas were on track to be achieved: children enrolled in preschool; employment of people aged 25–64 years; reduction of young people in detention; and Aboriginal and Torres Strait Islander land rights. Eight other areas showed some improvement while three areas were going backwards.[68]

While Closing the Gap is an important initiative, the *gradual* nature of the program has ignored the need for radical action in most of the target areas. In 2022, an ABC-TV *Four Corners* investigation revealed that three young Indigenous women who suffered from severe rheumatic heart disease (RHD) died in the space of one year after seeking help at Doomadgee Hospital. They were Betty Booth, aged 18, Shakaya George, aged 17 and Adele Sandy, aged 37. *Four Corners* reported that every time each of these women presented at the hospital's emergency department, they were sent home and told to take Panadol. A coroner stated: "RHD is 100 per cent preventable and is almost exclusively a disease of poverty and social disadvantage."[69] If governments were committed to exposing and punishing discrimination

---

67 Dana Morse, 30 November 2022, 'Closing the Gap Report Shows Four Targets Going Backwards as Experts Call for Efforts to "Empower Communities"', *ABC News*. <https://www.abc.net.au/news/2022-11-30/closing-the-gap-report-released/101713892>.
68 <https://www.pc.gov.au/closing-the-gap-data/annual-data-report/report>.
69 Louise Milligan, Naomi Selvaratnam and Lauren Day, 8 March 2022, 'Women Who Died After Going to Doomadgee Hospital with a Preventable Disease Were "Badly Let Down," Minister Says', *ABC News*. <https://www.abc.net.

and neglect as soon as they are identified in the health sector (similarly in employment and policing), the life expectancy and overall health of Indigenous people would be vastly improved. At the same time, the gap in economic status would be reduced and hope restored in many Aboriginal and Torres Strait Islander families.

Women's safety

After much agitation by feminists in the 1970s, the refuge movement saw the federal government providing minimal funding for the establishment of women's refuges/shelters in several areas in Australia. At least, it was a beginning. Then, the government of Prime Minister Bob Hawke responded to the need for more protection for women by instigating the National Agenda for Women in 1988. Since then, successive governments (federal, state and territory) have treated the safety of women and children as a serious issue and provided funding to support women's refuges, domestic violence services and sexual assault services in many parts of the country. Here I will mention just a few of the inquiries and initiatives undertaken since the 1980s:

1988 National Agenda for Women (an initiative of the Hawke Labor Government).

1990 National Committee on Violence against Women – delivered a national strategy (Hawke/Keating Labor Governments).

1993 United Nations Declaration on the Elimination of Violence against Women (Australia became a signatory to this declaration).

1996 National Domestic Violence Summit – established Partnerships Against Domestic Violence (PADV) (Howard Coalition Government).

---

au/news/2022-03-08/doomadgee-hospital-health-service-rhd-women-deaths/100887674>.

CHAPTER FOUR: CREATIVE WAYS OF AVOIDING THE TRUTH

2005 Women's Safety Agenda – a national multimedia campaign and the establishment of a 24-hour help line (Howard Coalition Government).

2008 National Council to Reduce Violence against Women and their Children (Rudd Labor Government). *Time for Action: the National Council's plan for Australia to reduce Violence against Women and their Children, 2009–2021.* Consisted of four three-year action plans.

2022 Draft National Plan to End Violence against Women and Children 2022–2032 (Morrison Coalition Government). Consisted of two five-year action plans.

The question must be asked: If governments place so much importance on this issue, so much time and energy in developing strategies and plans to keep women and children safe, so much funding, why are the statistics of men's violence against women still so stubbornly high? And why are women still being murdered by partners and ex-partners at the same – or even higher – alarming rate? I would venture to suggest that the answer lies in the reluctance of politicians and lawmakers to admit that this is a problem that must be owned by men. In the absence of that crucial acknowledgement, progress toward holding men to account for their violent attitudes and behaviour is so gradual as to be almost non-existent. Gradualism must be replaced by an honest acknowledgement of the facts together with radical action to change sexual inequality.

These three areas of perennial concern – aged care, Indigenous wellbeing and women's safety – are used here to illustrate the point that while gradualism is often employed by governments to give the appearance that something is being done to remedy stressful life experiences, it does in fact facilitate the avoidance of truth. If governments genuinely sought to confront the truth, radical action would follow.

Equalism

In the 1960s and 1970s, the Movements for Women's Liberation, Black Liberation and Gay Liberation (as they were named at the time) called for equality and justice. Women and men, disempowered because of their membership of these communities, demanded that they be treated equally with the rest of society. Then, as time passed, it became apparent to them that equality was not enough. There had to be equity and an acknowledgement of the effects of hate speech and vilification, physical and emotional violence, disadvantage in employment and the various levels of poverty caused by such discrimination.

Seemingly well-meaning members of the mainstream would brag about their commitment to equality between Indigenous and non-Indigenous people by declaring "I never see colour" when, in fact, colour is exactly what they must see. If members of the dominant white group close their eyes to the colour of another person's skin, they will never be in a position to acknowledge their own privilege, nor the discrimination that that person experiences every day of their lives.

In the referendum conducted in Australia in October 2023, aimed at altering the constitution to include a Voice to parliament for Indigenous Australians, there was a concerted effort by some (Indigenous and non-Indigenous) to encourage a 'No' vote. While some of the reasons put forward seemed to be well considered and credible, those protesting on the basis of equalism were less so. The lies and disinformation that flooded the right-wing media (including social media) were designed, it seemed, to create fear and confusion so that citizens would opt for the safety of the status quo and vote against the change.

Enquiries and polls taken both in the lead-up to the referendum and post-referendum reveal that 'equalism' played a significant role in its defeat. If one group, that is, Indigenous

CHAPTER FOUR: CREATIVE WAYS OF AVOIDING THE TRUTH

Australians, gets special mention in the constitution, it was argued, it will put members of that group above the rest. Equality demands that no one group is singled out for special mention. Indeed, the argument put forward by one young non-Indigenous politician married to an Indigenous woman was that a 'yes' vote in the referendum would cause his marriage to be unequal. His wife would be placed above him.[70] Such arguments are only plausible when the two people in question begin at the same place. In this particular case, the young politician was already two rungs higher than his wife: one, because he is a man and she is a woman; and two, because he is non-Indigenous and she is Indigenous. The referendum's aim of injecting some equity into the relationship between Australia's first people and the white majority was foiled by people's commitment to equalism.

In a similar way to non-Indigenous people saying "I never see colour," well-meaning men too can sometimes be heard to say: "When interviewing for a job (or when preselecting for a political party), I never think of a person's sex. Women and men are the same." Again, many men are well-intentioned when they stand up for equality in that way, but a woman's sex is exactly what they must see so that all the discrimination, all the physical and sexual violence, all the silencing, all the disadvantage that goes with being a woman in patriarchal society can be factored in to their decision-making.

Equalism is a word I am using here to describe a system of belief based on the misunderstanding/misinterpretation/ lie that 'equality' erases the need to respond to the effects of discrimination. In addition to those who are well-meaning but blind to the need for a more nuanced understanding of the weakness of equality as an aim, there are those who deliberately use 'equality' as a means of preserving the status quo. This is

---

70   <https://www.philthompson.com.au/the-voice/>.

particularly evident in relation to the issues around men's violence against women in the home. Regardless of statistics from reputable studies showing that the overwhelming numbers of perpetrators of domestic and family violence are men,[71] there persists in society the belief that women are just as violent as men. Men's rights groups peddle the lie that men need to be protected from women's violence in the home, and a society in the grip of equalism desperately wants to believe the lie.

An alarming fact is that when a woman or a concerned neighbour calls the police to attend a home where domestic violence is occurring and the woman is in need of protection, far too often the woman herself is identified by the police as the perpetrator of violence and charged with domestic violence offences. In many cases, the violent man has had time to settle himself down and concentrate on his image management. Then, when the police arrive, he presents as a calm, rational person who may have a scratch on him from his partner's attempt to protect herself, while the woman may be crying, shaking with fear and rage, and unable to speak. The police, already believing the lies about equality peddled by men's rights advocates, are primed to believe him. The effects of the misidentification of women as perpetrators of domestic violence have been far-reaching. Women who have suffered years of violence and humiliation at the hands of their partner find themselves in court charged with domestic violence offences. Some have had their children declared unsafe and subsequently removed by child safety officers, while others have seen courts grant custody of their children to violent fathers.

---

71   Australian Bureau of Statistics, 5 July 2018, 'Corrective Services Family and Domestic Violence Data Project: Discussion of Findings'. <https://www.abs.gov.au/statistics/people/crime-and-justice/corrective-services-family-and-domestic-violence-data-project-discussion-findings/latest-release>.

Feminist researchers and domestic violence workers have long called for a more accurate understanding of the coercive control male perpetrators use in their relationships over long periods (Hill 2019, Chapter 7). Alarmed at the increasing number of women wrongly arrested as perpetrators and later murdered by their husbands/partners, the Queensland Government instigated the Queensland Domestic and Family Violence Death Review in 2017. One of the recommendations from that review was that police and the courts improve their practice in identifying the "person most in need of protection." Australia's National Research Organisation for Women's Safety (ANROWS) followed up on the Queensland Government's Death Review recommendation and, following extensive research, presented the results in a paper titled, *Accurately identifying the 'person most in need of protection' in domestic and family violence law* (Australia's National Research Organisation for Women's Safety 2020).

Another worrying effect of equalism in relation to family law relates to the custody of children after separation and divorce. The government led by Prime Minister John Howard responded to the concerns of men's rights groups by changing parenting laws in 2006 to a presumption of equal shared parental responsibility. This has been interpreted by most people, including many judges and magistrates, to mean 50/50 shared care – children living 50% of the time with one parent and 50% with the other. Such an arrangement is extremely disruptive to children, many of whom find themselves shuffled week to week between two homes. Also, it presumes that both parents are responsible adults with the best interests of their children at heart. It also puts to one side any history of violence from one parent to the other or any history of abuse of the children. It presumes also that neither parent abuses alcohol or drugs in which case the children would be in need of protection. In many cases, the presumption that a 50/50 parental arrangement is in the best interests of the child does not stand up to the truth test. Zoe Rathus, Senior Lecturer at the Griffith University Law School, questions the use of the legal tool of 'presumption' and reminds her colleagues that "a presumption is a legal fiction and legal fictions become dangerous when their fictitious nature is forgotten" (Rathus 2010). In other words, it cannot and should not be presumed that a 50/50 arrangement, i.e., equality, is good for children.

A whole new area of concern for the wellbeing of women has opened up in recent years with an aggressive cohort of trans activists insisting that men who have decided to become women should have equal access to every space that has, until now, been reserved for women. Since the tradition of reserving separate spaces for women (women's rest rooms, women's change rooms, women's prisons, etc.) has existed in acknowledgement of the fact that women need to be kept safe from the predatory behaviour of some men, it is beyond belief that governments and community leaders are now putting women's safety aside in favour of the desire that men who are living as women have to feel equal, even in those cases where the men are still "biologically and legally male."[72]

The prison system is one arena where equalism is clearly working against the safety of women. In California, the purpose of *The Transgender Respect, Agency and Dignity Act* (2021) was to respond to reports of transgender 'women' being raped in male prisons by ruling that male prisoners who identify as trans be housed in women's prisons. Since the law was enacted, hundreds of men have applied for transfers to women's prisons, and authorities admit that they have no way of knowing who

---

72   <https://insidetime.org/trans-women-can-go-to-womens-jails-court-rules/>.

CHAPTER FOUR: CREATIVE WAYS OF AVOIDING THE TRUTH

is genuinely seeking to transition and who is not. Women are asking: Where is the compassion for women prisoners who are being harassed and raped by biologically intact males living in women's prisons? In November 2021, the Women's Liberation Front sued the California Department of Corrections and Rehabilitation alleging that this Bill "violates the Constitution by forcing women to be housed with male convicts who claim to be transgender." The transfers of trans women with male genitalia, they state, "have resulted in intimidation, sexual harassment, physical assaults, and sexual assaults committed by the men against female inmates."[73]

In Australia, too, women prisoners are concerned. Residents of the Dame Phyllis Frost Correctional Centre in Victoria have sent a written petition to authorities following the imprisonment of a trans person with a 'working penis'. They feel "threatened, unsafe, distressed and traumatised," they wrote. In the petition, they give reasons for their fear: He "has been convicted and is currently serving a sentence for the violent sexual assault of a woman in Victoria." This same man also "served a term of incarceration in Europe for the sexual assault of a six-year old female child" (Pahani 2022).

In 1993, Paul Denyer was arrested and charged on three counts of murder and one charge of abduction. The charges of murder, for which he plead guilty, were for the brutal killings of 18-year-old Elizabeth Stevens, 22-year-old Debbie Fream and 17-year-old Natalie Russell in the suburb of Frankston in Melbourne. He was sentenced to three consecutive sentences of life imprisonment with a non-parole period of 30 years. During the early years of his imprisonment, Denyer changed

---

[73] <https://www.lifesitenews.com/news/californias-transgender-policies-led-to-sexual-assaults-traumatization-of-female-prisoners-lawsuit-says/>.

his name to Paula and identified as a transgender woman but was refused permission by prison authorities to wear make-up, receive so-called 'sex reassignment surgery' or legally alter his name. Thankfully, his attempt to be moved to a women's prison also failed. Denyer became eligible for parole in 2023 but his application was denied. Writer Vikki Petraitis has researched Denyer's case extensively and wrote *The Frankston Murders: The True Story of Serial Killer Paul Denyer* (Petraitis 1995). She revisited the case more recently (Petraitis 2023) and developed *The Frankston Murders Podcast* as Denyer's parole bid was underway.

Men competing in women's sport is another area in which the belief in equalism is creating an unfair situation for women. Women athletes who have reached peak performance after years of training are in danger of losing out to someone who has the body and muscle structure of a man.

Equalism rests on the simplistic belief that equality is always positive when, in fact, it often serves to hide the truth by ignoring the need to go beneath the surface and discover the full impact every call for equality has on women. Proponents of equalism, the pursuit of equality at any cost, seem not to be bothered by the fact that the cost is usually borne by women.

Whataboutism

The Oxford Dictionary describes whataboutism as "the technique or practice of responding to an accusation or difficult question by making a counter-accusation or raising a different issue." It is a rhetorical manoeuvre, or a red herring, used by those seeking to avoid a topic that has the potential to cause them some discomfort. It is used in political confrontations, social situations and, also, in personal relationships.

CHAPTER FOUR: CREATIVE WAYS OF AVOIDING THE TRUTH

As alluded to earlier, one of President Donald Trump's memorable whataboutisms was his response to the devastating fatal attack at a white supremacist 'Unite the Right' rally in Charlottesville in August 2017. Without warning, a car driven by a member of one of the white supremacist groups ploughed into a group of counter-demonstrators, killing one woman. Altogether that day, there were three people dead and 35 injured. Attorney General Jeff Sessions condemned the violence and said:

> The violence and deaths in Charlottesville strike at the heart of American law and justice. When such actions arise from racial bigotry and hatred, they betray our core values and cannot be tolerated (Campbell and Mathias 2017).

In contrast, President Trump's response was a classic example of whataboutism. When asked about the incident at a press conference, he said:

> ... it was a horrible thing to watch. But there is another side. What about the alt-left that came charging at, as you say, the alt-right? ... You had a group on one side that was bad. You had a group on the other side that was also very violent (Fallon 2017).

Another example of whataboutism in the political arena was Australian Prime Minister Scott Morrison's attempt in 2021 to deflect questions by News Corporation journalist Andrew Clennell about reports of sexual harassment in Parliament House. Following reports by several women about the harassment they had experienced, journalists were intent on asking Mr Morrison what he was doing to change the situation. His response to Andrew Clennell was an expression of his frustration at being held responsible:

> You'd be aware that in your own organisation that there is a person who had had a complaint made against them for harassment of a woman in a women's toilet, and that matter is

being pursued by your own HR department … So let's not, all of us who sit in glass houses here, start getting into that.

A few hours later, the chairman of News Corp., Michael Miller, made it known that the Prime Minister had totally misrepresented an exchange that had occurred between two of his company's employees. There was a verbal exchange, he said, but it was "about a workplace-related issue, it was not of a sexual nature, it did not take place in a toilet and neither person made a complaint." The Prime Minister, embarrassed that his attempted whataboutism had backfired, issued a statement deeply regretting his "insensitive response" (Doran 2021).

Whataboutism is also used occasionally on the international stage. In November 2020, China's foreign ministry spokesman Zhao Lijian resurrected information from a four-year-old Australian investigation into the conduct of Australian Special Forces soldiers in Afghanistan. Out of the blue, he tweeted: "shocked by murder of Afghan civilians and prisoners by Australian soldiers" and included a fake image of an Australian soldier appearing to cut the throat of a young civilian. A report by the Australian Strategic Policy Institute (ASPI) concluded that the only explanation for the foreign ministry spokesman's action in resurrecting and misrepresenting the findings of the Australian investigation was to deflect attention from criticism of China over their treatment of Uyghurs. ASPI actually called it a clear example of whataboutism.[74]

Other examples of whataboutism are those that occur following every protest march or rally or demonstration raising issues of discrimination and injustice:

---

[74] This is not to deny that some Australian soldiers are guilty of having committed war crimes in Afghanistan but, rather, that Zhao Lijian's reference to it together with his use of a fake image was a clear example of whataboutism.

CHAPTER FOUR: CREATIVE WAYS OF AVOIDING THE TRUTH

Black Lives Matter marches – *What about white lives? Don't they matter?*

Women's marches against men's violence – *What about women's violence against men? They're just as bad.*

#MeToo revelations – *What about the way she behaved? What about her past history? She's not innocent either.*

Waititoutism

The fourth 'ism' I want to touch on is one that I have named waititoutism. Waititoutism describes a tactic governments in democratic countries use to great effect when pressure is on them to deal with problems that are not on their current list of priorities. They simply wait till the media cycle moves on to something else and the attention of the public is drawn in another direction.

Consider a fairly common situation where huge numbers of people are involved in a protest action. There is unrelenting questioning from journalists together with public anger and calls for justice to be done in relation to that particular issue but very little actually changes as a result. In June 2020, for example, tens of thousands of people marched in Black Lives Matter protests in Australia demanding an end to Indigenous deaths in custody. It was hoped and expected that the Royal Commission into Black Deaths in Custody in 1991 would go a long way toward preventing such tragedies but in April 2021, 30 years after the Royal Commission, it was reported that there had been 474 deaths in custody over that period.[75] How can it be that after

---

75   Lorena Allam, Calla Wahlquist, Nick Evershed and Miles Herbert, 9 April 2021, 'The 474 Deaths Inside: Tragic Toll of Indigenous Deaths in Custody Revealed', *The Guardian Australia*. <https://www.theguardian.com/australia-news/2021/apr/09/the-474-deaths-inside-rising-number-of-indigenous-deaths-in-custody-revealed>.

regular, strong and emotional protests over many years, nothing at all has changed? It is because governments of all stripes have become adept at steeling themselves against protests. They know that all they have to do is 'wait it out' until protesters resume their day-to-day lives and the media cycle moves on, at which time they can breathe freely again without the inconvenience of having to address the racial discrimination endemic in Australian society.

Similarly, men's violence against women continues apace. As already discussed, governments have, in recent years, seen the need to provide funding to services working to keep women and children safe but are resistant to pressure to focus on changing the behaviour of the men who perpetrate the violence. Even though the statistics of women seeking protection against their violent partners, and women being murdered by partners or ex-partners, have not reduced, governments still resist the call to declare men's violence against women a national emergency. Every protest action is met with a 'wait it out' response. Also, men who rape and sexually harass women continue to do so with impunity, while governments and legal institutions resist the pressure to hold men accountable. Again the tactic seems to be: 'wait it out' and it will pass.

In between high-profile campaigns like Australia's Black Lives Matter marches that occurred following the police murder of George Floyd in the United States, or March4Justice protests following the alleged rape of Brittany Higgins in Australia's Parliament House, a kind of collective amnesia seems to set in. When governments employ the tactic of waititoutism, and set up yet another inquiry, the moment is lost. Anger subsides and people forget. Nothing changes until the next high-profile murder or rape, and the whole process starts again: angry protests – media attention – official inquiry – government inaction – no change.

CHAPTER FOUR: CREATIVE WAYS OF AVOIDING THE TRUTH

Hideandseekism

The fifth and final ism draws attention to the extent that secrecy is used by governments and high profile companies to hide the truth from citizens, and the difficulty people encounter when they seek to break through the wall of silence that has been erected. Freedom of Information legislation (FOI) is meant to enable democratic access to information but delays, cost and large redactions often render the seeking pointless.

Rex Patrick, an Australian senator representing South Australia from 2017 to 2022, makes the point that transparency is a critical element of a representative democracy and that, without transparency, citizens cannot properly participate in the government of their country. While in the Senate, he threatened to take the Freedom of Information Commissioner to court over the lengthy delays in responding to his FOI requests. "If people are to engage in democracy," he said, "they have to be informed … (but) to be able to participate you need access to timely and up-to-date info." Expressing a serious concern shared by many, he added: "Often you will find there is a close correlation between secrecy and incompetence and corruption. That's why you want to have access to information" (Kelly 2021).

Another concern raised by Patrick was that, when one's FOI request is finally granted, the sometimes lengthy redactions can render a document useless. Often, they "block out the entire document and only reveal what they think is acceptable to release," he said. Denis Muller, senior research fellow at Melbourne University's Centre for Advancing Journalism, spoke of his own experience of redactions. "The public service plays all sorts of tricks," he said. "Once they redacted every word except the conjunctions and definite articles" (Kelly 2021).

In 2022, Rex Patrick made the decision not to seek re-election to the Senate, but went ahead with his challenge in the federal court to the lengthy delays involved in the handling of FOI requests. Delay is the "enemy of FOI," he said (Knaus 2023).

Bill Browne, Director for Democracy and Accountability at The Australia Institute agrees. "Democracies depend on transparency, but Australia's Freedom of Information systems are not giving the public the information they are entitled to." Instead, the system is "delaying, obfuscating and holding back information" (Knaus 2023).

To sum up, I quote from the Transparency Warrior website reiterating the point made by Rex Patrick:

> ... transparency is a critical element of a representative democracy. Without transparency citizens cannot properly participate in democracy – and the likelihood of corruption or maladministration occurring increases.[76]

Focusing back on the obsession some governments seem to have with secrecy, an over-used excuse for keeping the general population in ignorance are the words 'national security'. While it is accepted that governments do sometimes need to keep confidences in relation to international affairs and potential trade deals, this particular excuse for secrecy is used to cover a wide range of situations and, whether it is true or not in any given instance, most people seem willing to accept that there could be much more going on under the surface than their government is willing to divulge at that time.

Another slogan used by the conservative governments of Tony Abbott, Malcolm Turnbull and Scott Morrison over a number of years was 'on-water matters'. When many Australian citizens were expressing concern about the government's treatment of asylum-seekers who came by boat, the issue of 'on-water matters' was presented as a matter of 'national security' (Slezak 2016). Consequently, questions from concerned citizens

---

76 <https://transparencywarrior.com.au/about/>.

CHAPTER FOUR: CREATIVE WAYS OF AVOIDING THE TRUTH

about the welfare of this particular cohort of asylum-seekers almost always came up against a wall of silence.

The secrecy that has the potential to destroy democracy extends, also, to governments' dealings with powerful companies who are used by governments as consultants in numerous areas. In recent times, successive governments have deliberately slimmed down the public service in favour of awarding contracts to consulting companies to do the kinds of work the public service used to do, but the relationship between Australia's federal government and the consulting firm PricewaterhouseCoopers (PwC) has recently been embroiled in a very big scandal. A global professional services company, PwC provides accounting and consulting services and its biggest Australian client is the federal government who awards the firm contracts for consulting services on defence, federal police, education, social security and transport spending. While the scandal is still shrouded in secrecy, some facts have come to light. It seems that PwC's international tax expert Peter-John Collins was approached by Joe Hockey in his role as federal treasurer in the Abbott government (2013–2015) to assist in developing a law "to stop major companies, particularly tech giants, from shifting their profits away from higher-taxing countries like Australia to others with lower tax rates." In setting up the contract, the federal government required Mr Collins to sign "multiple confidentiality agreements which specifically stated that the knowledge could not be disclosed." The scandal that has come to light is that Mr Collins did, indeed, share the government's secrets with his colleagues at PwC. They, in turn, shared this secret knowledge with their partners who then "approached at least 14 global companies with a plan on how to dodge the new tax laws." PwC saw it as an opportunity to help big multinational companies avoid paying more tax in Australia and at the same time to attract new clients (Ainsworth 2023).

As the details of the scandal came to light early in 2023, Prime Minister Anthony Albanese and Treasurer Jim Chalmers expressed their anger and disappointment at the enormity of the breach of trust. Using words like 'ropeable' and 'furious', Dr Chalmers said:

> I am personally, the government, I think the country is absolutely filthy about what's happened with PwC. We want to be able to consult in good faith with the business community on changes that have the capacity to affect them.
>
> We cannot have a repeat of this absolutely appalling episode, where people were monetising government secrets (Elton 2023).

This is an example of how the secrecy involved in relationships between governments and the business community can allow corruption to take a foothold. As this scandal came to light through the efforts of the Australian Taxation Office, those politicians who had been kept in the dark began to insist on transparency. Several senators expressed outrage at the fact that PwC was going to conduct a review of its own behaviour and publish a summary of the findings of the review. Labor senator Deborah O'Neill called it "an inside job ... They are still not coming clean," she said. "That the release of information will be controlled by PwC shows ... the review does not have any credibility." Greens senator Barbara Pocock said the inquiry was "totally inappropriate ... Promising to release a summary of the findings is not the same thing as making the findings available to the public." Liberal senator Andrew Bragg called the scandal "an abomination" (Tadros 2023). Following the revelations, and outraged at the lack of accountability, the senate immediately launched an inquiry into the use of consultants by the federal government.

It is clear, as this chapter has demonstrated, that politics often seems to be an exercise in how to manage appearance, how to

CHAPTER FOUR: CREATIVE WAYS OF AVOIDING THE TRUTH

appear to be measuring up to people's expectations while at the same time delaying action and deceiving those who trust their leaders. Some say that this is 'clever' politics but, if truth be told, it is grubby politics, a willingness to use lies and deceit to achieve one's own political ends. The deception inherent in gradualism, equalism, whataboutism, waititoutism and hideandseekism goes against democratic principles and has no place in any country purporting to be a democracy.

CHAPTER FIVE

Individualism, Populism and Identity Politics

This is the third of three chapters in which I highlight some of the circumstances threatening the survival of democracy. In Chapter Three, the focus was on the prevalence of lies and disinformation in today's politics and society, while Chapter Four sought to expose some of the 'clever' and 'creative' tactics politicians and other leaders use to deceive us. Here, in this chapter, I move my focus from the political arena to the personal and draw attention to the damaging effects of individualism. The claim I make is that individualism, a central feature of liberal democracy, is out of control. From a discussion of the excesses caused by liberalism's focus on the individual, it will be a natural progression, then, to discuss two developments closely related to those excesses. They are populism and identity politics.

The fact that democracy is in crisis has been obvious to feminist scholars and activists for decades, as evidenced in my focus on feminist concerns spelled out in Chapter One. But the crisis has now intensified to the point that a range of philosophers, political scientists, sociologists and others are expressing serious fears for its survival (see Chapter Three). There seems to be a general consensus among those writing about the crisis that what today's democracy needs is a radical injection of truth with the aim of confronting the excesses of individualism and restoring a balance between individual rights and social responsibilities. Most democracies in the west are liberal democracies and, in the opinion of many radical feminists, therein lies the problem. Liberalism, with its emphasis on individualism, is eating away at important democratic values such as: a sense of community, freedom of speech for all, the sharing of ideas, a willingness to compromise, inclusion, justice and acceptance of the rule of law.

To highlight the extent to which individualism puts the very foundations of democracy at risk, it is important to take a closer look at liberalism.

Liberalism – earlier times

As mentioned in the Introduction, liberalism emerged during the Age of Enlightenment in the seventeenth century as a movement aimed at replacing the divine right of kings and hereditary privilege with representative democracy and the rule of law. While it is impossible to say exactly when liberalism was born, the writings of men like Thomas Hobbes (1588–1679), Benedict de Spinoza (1632–1677) and John Locke (1632–1704) introduced many of its ideas, the central themes of which are individualism, freedom and reason.

Originally, the freedoms of liberalism were for white men only and, to be more precise, for white men who were property owners. All other groups – white men of the working and middle classes, women, Indigenous peoples and people of ethnic origin – had to fight long and hard to be allowed access to the freedoms enjoyed by white men of the upper class. While many gains have been made through determined protest, the aim of genuine inclusion is still a long way off.

Historically, it would seem that proponents of liberalism have had a great capacity for self-delusion. The Declaration of

CHAPTER FIVE: INDIVIDUALISM, POPULISM AND IDENTITY POLITICS

Independence in the US stated, on 4 July 1776: "We hold these truths to be self-evident, that all men are created equal," but it was not until 3 February 1870, when the 15th Amendment was ratified, that African-American men were granted the right to vote. African-American women had to wait, as did all women, until they were granted the right to vote in 1920. Even then, it was not until the *Voting Rights Act* of 1965 that African-Americans' right to register and vote was fully protected.

In Australia, there existed the same self-delusion. Australia was established as a British colony in 1901. It was a parliamentary democracy with free elections, freedom of political participation, freedom of speech and so on. Women were granted the vote in 1902. While voting was compulsory for 'everyone', it actually allowed for the exclusion of Indigenous people. In fact, Indigenous men and women were not even counted as citizens of Australia until the census of 1967.

Right from the start, the egalitarian nature of Australia's liberal democracy was a lie. In addition to the exclusion of Indigenous people, there was the *Immigration Restriction Act* of 1901, commonly known as the White Australia Policy, which stayed in place until 1966 when Prime Minister Harold Holt began dismantling it (though not for Asians). It was not until 1973 that the government of Prime Minister Gough Whitlam renounced the policy totally and established a policy of multi-culturalism.

Liberalism today

It will be interesting to see how social historians categorise these early decades of the twenty-first century. Feminists, sociologists, ethicists and other social justice analysts express dismay at what is occurring. As Michael Sandel, political philosopher and Professor of Government Theory at Harvard University Law

School, asked recently: "What sense can we make of our current political moment?" (Sandel 2020).

There is no doubt that many are puzzled about the current political situation. The old categories of left and right, liberal and conservative, good and bad, no longer seem appropriate, especially when some of the things that many have grown up believing are 'good' and to be aimed for (e.g. education) are now criticised by a large number of people and labelled elitist and 'bad'. These confusing times have caused some academics to express considerable disenchantment with liberalism.

Adrian Pabst, Professor of Politics at the University of Kent, explores the possibility of a postliberal politics that, he explains, is not anti-liberal but, rather, a correction of the errors that have developed:

> Genuine postliberalism draws on the best liberal traditions but corrects liberal errors and excesses such as individualism, untrammelled capitalism or identity politics. Its organizing principles are community, mutual markets, ethical enterprise and the common purposes around which people associate (Pabst 2021, p. ix).

Feminists, too, are expressing concern about liberalism's growing focus on the individual and some are quick to make the connection between individualism and neoliberalism. Meagan Tyler is critical of mainstream feminism's shift in focus from analysing social and political systems "to a more psychologised, individual understanding of a freely-chosen sense of self."[77]

Similarly, a panel of speakers in the UK – Nimco Ali, Kathleen Stock, Mary Harrington and Nina Power – refer to liberal feminism as "a liberal doctrine that prioritises freedom above all else." Under the title "Beyond the failures of liberal feminism,"

---

[77] Meagan Tyler, 8 March 2021, 'Can Feminism Be Saved from Identity Politics?' *ABC Religion & Ethics*. <https://www.abc.net.au/religion/can-feminism-be-saved-from-identity- politics/11646084>.

CHAPTER FIVE: INDIVIDUALISM, POPULISM AND IDENTITY POLITICS

they discuss the failures and then go on to contemplate a new form of postliberal feminism (2020).[78]

In an attempt to understand how we arrived at this point, it might be helpful to look back over recent history and try to identify the stages that have led to this moment. Beginning immediately after World War II, the post-war years (late 1940s and 1950s) emphasised conservative family values. Society was intent on healing the nation and supporting the men who had returned from fighting a terrible war. Women who had been needed in the workforce were no longer needed and so were sent back to their homes to fulfil the roles of wife and mother. Men returning from the war had to be taken care of and the nation was in want of more babies, so women's role was mandated.

The next stage (1960s and 1970s) represented a period of radical social demands. Women, in particular, were suffocating under a regime of traditional patriarchal values and insisted on coming out from under the repressive, restrictive demands on them. This was a period of rebellion, as the strength of the Women's Liberation Movement demonstrated. Social justice movements pointed to the second-class status of women, of racial minorities and of other groups who were disempowered by the system, and demanded that such discrimination be stamped out. It was an exciting time, full of hope that justice would prevail.

Then came a change in focus (1980s and 1990s) from radical social demands to a more conservative individual focus. Globalisation and neoliberal economic theories took centre stage and citizens were encouraged (one might say, indoctrinated) to focus on themselves, on improving their own ability to compete and increase their own individual opportunities with the aim of

---

78 Mary Harrington, Nimco Ali, Nina Power and Kathleen Stock, 17 December 2020, 'Beyond the Failures of Liberal Feminism', *Republica*. <https://www.respublica.org.uk/event/beyond-the-failures-of-liberal-feminism/>.

being winners and not losers. It was an attractive change to many but the focus on one's individual self was often at the expense of concern for others. Indeed, the idea was that individuals should *compete* with other individuals, rather than nurturing any desire for cooperation and sharing.

Then, at the turn of the millennium (2000s to the present), the emphasis on the individual continued, with a society encouraged to believe that the freedoms afforded by liberalism were one's own individual freedoms. Many people interpreted that to mean freedom to say and do as they liked with little respect for the rights of others; freedom to troll and vilify others; freedom to express opinions that had little basis in fact; and so on. Everyone, buoyed by the opinions freely given by peers on social media, was an authority, and had no need for facts derived from social analysis by reputable sources.

When freedom of the individual is prioritised above all else, the central truths of democracy become lost in the pursuit of one's own opinions and aspirations.

Liberalism's excesses

Unrestrained freedom inevitably results in excesses, as the following discussion will reveal. From the many options available to me, I focus attention on the excesses of liberalism under three headings: speech, greed and violence.

Speech

The most misrepresented concept in liberalism today surely is the principle of free speech. Instead of a freedom enabling honest and robust communication, thereby enriching society, it has become for many a licence to lie, vilify and threaten, with the aim of silencing or 'cancelling' others. Indeed, it is a brave person who dares give a serious opinion on social media because an

CHAPTER FIVE: INDIVIDUALISM, POPULISM AND IDENTITY POLITICS

honest comment is so often met with ridicule, insults and threats to life and limb. In addition to bringing communities together as was hoped when social media first appeared, it has also become an instrument used to drive people apart – a platform on which people quickly find their 'tribe' (see Chapter Three) and learn from other members how to bring down members of other tribes.

Maria Ressa of *Rappler* writes passionately and convincingly about the "absence of the rule of law in the virtual world" and the damage that has done to democracy. "Impunity online naturally led to impunity offline," she said:

> What I have witnessed and documented over the past decade is technology's godlike power to infect each of us with a virus of lies, pitting us against one other, igniting, even creating, our fears, anger, and hatred, and accelerating the rise of authoritarians and dictators around the world (Ressa 2022, p. 4).

To illustrate the way the speech of social media is destroying democracy, Ressa points to the elections in the Philippines on 9 May 2022. The election was won by Ferdinand Marcos Jr, "the only son and namesake of the dictator Ferdinand Marcos, who declared martial law in 1972 and stayed in power for nearly 21 years." Referring to the election as "a showcase for the impact of disinformation on social media," she describes a situation where the dictator Marcos was transformed "from a pariah into a hero." The disinformation networks "helped change history in front of our eyes" (pp. 5–6).

In addition to spreading disinformation, social media is also the platform most often used to bully and harass those one disagrees with. Shutting people up is the aim rather than encouraging the free expression of ideas. Democracy's marketplace of ideas, robust discussion, agreeing to differ, searching for compromises have all been replaced by cancel culture and de-platforming in liberalism's new iteration.

Cancel culture is a term used to describe the situation occurring today where people are 'cancelled', reputations destroyed, livelihoods lost, all because they may have used the wrong pronoun or not sounded sufficiently sympathetic toward the plight of racial minorities, or not sounded dismissive enough of someone accused of abuse. Waleed Aly, in an important essay on this topic, described what he called "the atmosphere of the moment":

> … this sense that a wild reckoning is afoot; that punishment and intimidation are beginning to stand in for persuasion or teaching; that a tweet here or a comment there is sufficient basis to define a person's entire character; that people are no longer permitted first drafts of their ideas and themselves before being assailed; that even the passage of decades offers no protection; that reputations built over a lifetime can be broken down in an instant (Aly 2020, p. 3).

Stunned by the fierce reaction, a victim of cancel culture may apologise for the unintended hurt but forgiveness rarely comes because judgement is swift and the 'offending' person has already been cancelled. The fact that there is no room for explanation, discussion, apology or restoration of relationships puts cancel culture outside the orbit of liberal democracy.

It used to be that those on the left might cancel those on the right and vice versa but today, cancel culture occurs left against left, right against right, older lefties against younger lefties, feminists against feminists, leaving much confusion and pain in its wake.

Feminists find themselves 'cancelled' today most often in relation to transgender issues. Many well-known and well-respected feminists who were in high demand to speak at universities and conferences all around the world find now that

CHAPTER FIVE: INDIVIDUALISM, POPULISM AND IDENTITY POLITICS

they are de-platformed, denied the right to speak, because of an article or book they once wrote or an opinion they expressed that was not 100% in favour of everything the trans lobby is demanding. Janice G. Raymond, Julie Bindel, Sheila Jeffreys, Meghan Murphy, Germaine Greer, J. K. Rowling and many others are labelled TERFs[79] and banished forever. One wonders what happened to the principle of free speech that once was central to liberal democracy. Many feminists who have been de-platformed have made it clear that they do not hate individual men and women who decide to transition, but it makes no difference. If they 'liked' the wrong thing on Facebook (which is how the torrents of abuse started for J. K. Rowling) or expressed objections to the use of language that erases women, such as 'person with a front hole', 'chest-feeding' and 'birthing parent', the trans-lobby pounces and they are cancelled.

Janice G. Raymond has been in the sights of trans activists ever since she wrote her ground-breaking work *The Transsexual Empire* in 1979. In her latest book *Doublethink: A Feminist Challenge to Transgenderism* (2021), she gives many examples of radical feminists being silenced by universities, social media, government bodies and others. Here are a few examples.

Germaine Greer was boycotted from speaking at universities following the lecture she gave at Cardiff University in 2015 in which she said: "I don't believe a woman is a man without a cock." During question time, when challenged about the vulnerability of trans-identified people, she responded sensitively to the challenge and then reiterated: "I don't accept postoperative males as females" (in Raymond 2021, p. 191).

Julie Bindel has been no-platformed by the UK National Union of Students (NUS). Prior to a Lesbian, Gay, Bisexual, Transgender conference in 2011, the NUS stated: "This

---

79 Trans Exclusionary Radical Feminists.

conference believes that Julie Bindel is vile," demonstrating that their attack was not only against Bindel's opinions but also against her person (in Raymond 2021, p. 195).

When invited by staff (not the NUS) to debate a pornographer at Essex University, the usual kind of petition went around: "Ban Julie Bindel from campus, her presence on campus ... will be an act of violence." On the day of the debate, while Bindel was walking through campus with the pornographer (who for years had produced pornography exploiting and degrading women), they came upon a group of students who shouted words like "transphobe" and "violent" at her. Subsequently, Bindel commented on the fact that the pornographer could walk through that campus "with no dissent and no concern at all from these so-called feminists and pro-feminist students, and I'm being screamed at" (Bindel 2015).

Kathleen Stock, Professor of Philosophy at Sussex University, resigned her position at the university because the accusations and threats against her made it impossible for her to continue. Also, there was concern for her safety. She was accused of "creating an 'unsafe environment' by arguing against the trans dogma that men could self-identify as women and/or lesbians." She was "publicly branded as 'transphobic' by the Sussex students' union" and, later, when awarded an Order of the British Empire (OBE), "600 of Stock's peers from academic institutions in several countries criticized the decision to award her an OBE" by adding their names to an 'Open Letter Concerning Transphobia in Philosophy' (in Raymond 2021, p. 197).

Sheila Jeffreys, former Professor of Politics at the University of Melbourne, discusses in her autobiography *Trigger Warning: My Lesbian Feminist Life* (2020), some of the accusations made against her by trans activists and the demonstrations that were intended to make it difficult for her to continue her work.

CHAPTER FIVE: INDIVIDUALISM, POPULISM AND IDENTITY POLITICS

The harassment began in earnest, she says, following the release of her book *Gender Hurts: A Feminist Analysis of the Politics of Transgenderism* in 2014. She writes:

> The transgender rights movement was so influential by this time, that any challenge or criticism of their political ideology or practice was greeted with great fury and outrage such that the academy and many politicians and institutions of state were running scared. The flame-throwing power of the clearly male rage, blasted journalists, politicians and feminists into silence (Jeffreys 2020, p. 213).

Thankfully, Sheila Jeffreys will never be silenced. Consequently, transactivists did everything they could to sully her name. They wrote to her university accusing her of teaching 'hate speech', with a view to having her censored or worse. It never happened. They made plans to invade her lectures to express their rage. So great was their fury that Jeffreys became concerned for her safety on campus and sought the advice of university lawyers and campus security. Much later (2023), Holly Lawford-Smith, Associate Professor in Political Philosophy at the same university and author of *Gender-Critical Feminism* (Lawford-Smith 2022), also had to seek protection.

Janice G. Raymond recounts one of her own experiences, not with a university, but with government censorship in Oslo in 2013. After inviting her to speak "on the subject of prostitution and the Norwegian law against the purchasing of sexual activities," she said, the Ombuds Office disinvited her. She was informed that she had been excluded from the speakers' panel because of her views on transsexualism (Raymond 2021, p. 213).

Raymond also discusses the censorship that occurs on social media. Her experience, and that of many other feminists, is that *Wikipedia* "erases radical feminist views on transgender." Anything that is mildly critical of transgenderism is either edited or deleted altogether:

Forced censorship of content is rampant on Wikipedia, and the back and forth of principles involved in the undoing of radical feminist gender-critical content is based on clear bias. The sheer volume of edits made to gender critical content is dizzying (p. 206).

Censorship was also rife on *Twitter*. *Twitter* developed a 'Hateful Conduct' policy in 2018–2019 and while it was rarely enforced against those who made rape and death threats against women, it was strictly enforced against the "misgendering or deadnaming of transgender individuals."[80] Radical feminist and editor of the online feminist website *Feminist Current*, Canadian Meghan Murphy, incurred a life ban for saying "men are not women" (in Raymond 2021, p. 207).[81]

Cancel culture is ruthless and unforgiving. Its proponents are not satisfied simply to dismiss the 'offending' words and actions of a person but it is the person herself who must be punished, destroyed, eradicated – banished from the face of the earth, so to speak. Regardless of how much knowledge and experience a feminist may have in the fight against pornography, prostitution, trafficking, climate action, etc., once she says "a man can't be a woman" or "it's impossible to change sex" or "transwomen are transwomen" (as Nigerian feminist Chimamanda Adichie Ngozie said in an interview in 2017),[82] she is to be cancelled forever. Similarly, regardless of how much good a man may have done, how many lives may have been saved due to his discoveries

---

80 Twitter Help Center 2019.
81 When Elon Musk took over Twitter (now called X) Meghan Murphy's ban was lifted.
82 Jessica Taylor, 6 October 2022, 'Award-winning Novelist Chimamanda Ngozi Adichie Who Was Cancelled for Saying "Transwomen Are Transwomen" Insists She Will Continue to "Say What She Thinks" and Is Happy to "Accept the Consequences", *Daily Mail*. <https://www.dailymail.co.uk/femail/article-11286775/Chimamanda-Ngozi-Adichie-continue-say-thinks-accused-transphobia.html>.

as a medical scientist, once he says "the XX or XY chromosomes one is born with determines one's sex and cannot be changed," he is erased.[83]

In liberal democracies, freedom of speech has always occupied a central place. It is the principle that most distinguishes democratic from authoritarian regimes. Free expression, the right to protest, the expectation that one's words will be listened to and accepted as part of the debate on any issue, are all precious values in a democracy. It is true, as I have stated elsewhere, that some people have more access to speech than others and that is an inequality that must be put right (McLellan 2010), but there is, nevertheless, the expectation of free speech for all. The very idea of cancel culture is antithetical to democracy.

Greed

When neoliberalism became the preferred economic theory in democratic countries, greed featured more than it ever had before. The power of the market was prioritised and individual citizens were encouraged to play their part. If individuals could be influenced to believe that greed is good, they would be motivated to choose economic success as a guiding principle in their lives. Governments believed that if they could get more people to take risks, become shareholders, invest with a view to growing their portfolios, businesses would thrive and the national budget would benefit. Competition was encouraged and for many, greed became the 'ethic' to overshadow all other ethics. In the world of competition, when 'the survival of the fittest' is the mantra, the end often justifies the means and the most egregious things are done in the service of greed. Adrian

---

83 See the work of Colin Wright, Evolutionary Biologist and Academic Advisor at the Society for Evidence-based Gender Medicine. <https://www.realityslaststand.com/>.

Pabst refers to the "dehumanizing exploitation of contemporary capitalism" (Pabst 2021, p. 118).

Exploitation of the less powerful

Greed entrenches inequality. When a company decides to increase its profits by moving parts of its business offshore and employing people from poorer countries at a vastly reduced rate of pay, its original employees can be fired en masse, plunging many into financial hardship and even poverty. With profitmaking as the justification, that company's executives have no qualms about destroying the livelihoods of so many previously faithful employees nor about exploiting their new employees who may be simply grateful to have jobs.

While this is happening, CEOs of such companies seem quite happy to take home inflated salaries, often topped up by very generous bonuses. The salary of Qantas CEO Alan Joyce in 2022 was reported in this way: "Qantas CEO Alan Joyce has received a $2.27 million remuneration package but his pay is still well below pre-pandemic levels when he received an eye-watering $10.86 million in 2018."[84] CEO of Harvey Norman, Katie Page, received $3.5 million in 2020, plus bonuses.[85] In 2021, Afterpay co-founders Anthony Eisen and Nick Molnar took home a combined salary of $264.2 million, Macquarie's Shemara Wikramanayake, $14.7 million and Woolworth's Brad Banducci, $11.8 million. It is calculated that the "highest paid CEOs earn about 132 times more than the average worker in Australia."[86]

---

84 On retirement from Qantas in September 2023, Joyce's final pay (including shares and bonuses) was $22 million. See <https://www.sbs.com.au/news/article/qantas-ceo-alan-joyces-pay-rises-past-2-million/jn02hltvg>.
85 <https://www.channelnews.com.au/has-harvey-norman-revenues-started-to-slump-their-shares-have/>.
86 <https://www.peoplemattersglobal.com/news/leadership/top-10-highest-paid-ceos-in-australia-34714>.

CHAPTER FIVE: INDIVIDUALISM, POPULISM AND IDENTITY POLITICS

By way of comparison, the average hourly rate for an aged care worker in Australia (as at June 2023) is $22.80, and for a childcare worker $30.51.[87] Job Seeker (an unemployment benefit) for singles is $762.70 per fortnight and the aged pension for singles is $1,020.60 per fortnight.

That such inequality is tolerated (and increasing) in a democratic country, without government intervention, is testament to the fact that greed is accepted as the way to do business.

Wreaking havoc on the planet

Greed is the motivating force behind the fossil fuel industry's determination to ignore the scientific evidence that coal must be phased out if the planet is to survive the catastrophic effects of climate change. At COP26 in Glasgow in 2021, a commitment was reached to phase down the use of coal. Then, in 2022, at COP27 in Egypt, some countries wanted to go further and called for a commitment to phase out *all* fossil fuels, including gas, but agreement could not be reached. When the draft report was released, Joseph Sikulu of the Pacific Climate Warriors expressed his disappointment:

> The cover text released this morning does not represent the call from both the negotiating rooms as well as the civil society for a just, equitable and managed phase-out of all fossil fuels. Anything less than what we achieved in Glasgow will see Cop27 branded a failure by the world.[88]

COP28, held in Dubai in 2023 and attended by 97,000 people including 2,456 fossil-fuel lobbyists, ended with an agreement to 'transition away' from fossil fuels. For those hoping to see climate

---

[87] Pay scales differ from state to state.
[88] Sandra Laville and Bibi van der Zee, 17 November 2022, 'Draft Cop27 agreement fails to call for "phase-down" of all fossil fuels', *The Guardian*. <https://www.theguardian.com/environment/2022/nov/17/draft-cop27-agreement-fails-to-call-for-phase-down-of-all-fossil-fuels?ref=upstract.com>.

justice, this outcome was disappointing, to say the least. In the words of the authors of an article on the successes and failures of COP28, it was "not a resounding win for justice" (Donohue and Perry 2023).

For oil-rich, coal-rich, gas-rich countries, there is no doubt that phasing out fossil fuels in favour of renewables will come at a cost to them, but the survival of the planet demands that they heed the warnings of the Intergovernmental Panel on Climate Change and invest in alternatives sooner rather than later.

Wanton destruction of historical sites

When there is a profit to be made, greed enables people and companies to close their minds to the irreplaceable value of historical sites. Many Australians, Indigenous and non-Indigenous, are still mourning the loss of the Juukan Gorge rock shelters blown up by Rio Tinto in May 2020 to allow the company access to higher-grade iron ore. These were Aboriginal heritage sites dating back 46,000 years and now they are gone forever. The traditional owners of Juukan Gorge, the Puutu Kunti Kurrama and Pinikura peoples, acknowledge that Rio Tinto was able to destroy the sacred site because there was no law to prevent it, and call on State and Federal governments to amend the law so that such a tragedy never happens again. Clare Wright, Professor of History at LaTrobe University, lamented:

> In a matter of minutes, eight million tonnes of ore were ripped from the earth, and with them, 46,000 years of cultural heritage destroyed (Wright 2021).

Sexual exploitation of women

Greed, together with no small amount of misogyny, is the motivating force behind the ever-increasing violence against women portrayed by the pornography and prostitution industries. Dressed up as choices that women make, the reality is that women are exploited by pornographers and pimps so that men can experience the pleasure of 'relationships' with no mutual obligations. Also, women who are trafficked from one country to another are owned and dominated by the sex industry, often with no hope of escaping till the industry has used them up.

Of all the excesses of liberalism that exist in today's democracies, the sexual exploitation of women is the one that seems to enjoy the acceptance and approval of governments and many in the community. Men's sex right is accepted as a given and, as men's greed for sex grows, the expectation is that women will be there to service that greed – for very little remuneration and even less pleasure.

Violence

Sexual violence

I chose to position the sexual exploitation of women under the heading of 'greed' (above) because it represents the commodification of women for the financial gain of powerful industries, but it is appropriate also to discuss it under the heading violence. Pornography and prostitution, while presented by many as good for women, are actually practices that harm women, as I have illustrated earlier in this book.

The excesses of today's liberalism are no more obvious than in the increasing violence against women portrayed in pornography for the pleasure of men. It seems that there is no end to men's appetite for viewing violent acts performed on women, and Melinda Tankard Reist's 2022 book, *He Chose Porn over Me: Women Harmed by Men Who Use Porn*, reveals that many men are willing to give up hitherto decent relationships in favour of their right to consume such pornography (Tankard

Reist (ed.) 2022). Prostitution, too, puts women in harm's way, having to deal with men who sometimes seek to play out violent fantasies on women who are not their partners.

Another feature of today's liberalism is the use of sex dolls, which one feminist researcher has labelled "woman hating," as men do to dolls what they fantasise doing to real women. Caitlin Roper's book: *Sex Dolls, Robots and Woman Hating: The Case for Resistance*, describes a growing trend in the use of sex toys by men (Roper 2022).

The prevalence of rape and sexual harassment has been revealed by the #MeToo movement and, on a positive note, revealed in a way that has forced society to sit up and take notice. For years, feminists have written about their own and other women's experiences of sexual violence by men they worked with, socialised with, lived with, but it wasn't until the #MeToo movement that men realised they were being called to account for their abusive behaviour. Jess Hill described it appropriately when she said:

> At its heart, this is an accountability movement, one that dares to ask men the ugly question: what will it take for your kind to stop coercing, harassing, raping, and killing women? Of power, it demands: what will it take for you to stop protecting the men who perpetrate this?

Women are no longer content just to say: "*I was raped, but he is the one who raped me – and they are the ones who protected him*" (Hill 2021, p. 3).

It is way past time that the focus was on the rapist and on those who protect him, including all of society's systems developed for the precise purpose of protecting and diverting attention away from rapists. What was the victim wearing, had she been drinking, did she lure him into her trap, why didn't she say 'no' more convincingly ... all such questions miss the point. The point is that when a man is on trial for rape, it is he, the alleged rapist, who must be held to account for his behaviour, not the victim.

Violence in the community

Another worrying trend is the increase in men's violence against other men. Some parents express fears about their sons going out to meet up with their mates in the city or at nightclubs because of the prevalence of violent attacks by groups of young men on other men. Sometimes there is a racial element to the violence where a gang of white youths look to pick a fight with a lone Indigenous man or group of Indigenous men. Sometimes a gang of men from one ethnic group attacks a gang from a different ethnic group. There are examples of individual men innocently walking home after a night out being attacked and sometimes killed by a group of men looking for a fight. Alcohol and drugs are often involved in men's violent attacks but it would be wrong to blame substance abuse alone. Violent men are violent to other men because of their need for dominance.

Women have long since known that it is not safe for them to walk alone at night (or even to walk together with one or two women friends). Regardless of a woman's age, she is seen as fair game if she has the audacity to believe that it is her right to walk alone, day or night. The statistics of women being harassed, raped and sometimes murdered by men who are strangers are increasing. Consider this small selection of murders that occurred in Australia over the last 12 years:

- 2012 Jill Meagher, 29 years old. Raped and strangled while walking home along Sydney Road, Brunswick, in Melbourne.
- 2015 Masa Vukotic, 17 years old. Stabbed to death while out on her evening walk in Melbourne.
- 2018 Eurydice Dixon, 22 years old. Raped and murdered while walking home alone in Melbourne.

2018 Toyah Cordingly, 24 years old. Murdered while walking her dog on Wangetti Beach, north of Cairns.

2019 Aiia Maasarwe, 21 years old. Raped and murdered while walking home alone in Melbourne's northern suburbs.

2021 Jasmeen Kaur, 21 years old. Kidnapped while walking home from work and murdered. Her body was found in a shallow grave in Flinders Ranges in South Australia.

Violence in relationships

Domestic violence statistics reveal that it is overwhelmingly men who are violent toward their partners or ex-partners. When I worked as a counsellor at the North Queensland Domestic Violence Resource Service from 2013 to 2022, I often found myself thinking of Germaine Greer's words: "Women have no idea how much men hate them." The horrendous violence that so many men perpetrate against women in relationships, and after relationships end, is hard to comprehend. Why do they do it? Why are they not ashamed? And why are other men not outraged by the behaviour of their kind, enough to confront violent men and demand that the violence stops? Maybe it's because all men benefit from all women being reminded of how vulnerable they are in relationships with men.

Safe Steps, a family violence response centre supported by the Victorian government, has brought together on their website disturbing statistics on violence against women in Australia, gleaned from reports from such reputable institutions as the Australian Institute of Criminology, Australian Institute of Health and Welfare and the Australian Bureau of Statistics.

- On average, one woman a week is murdered by her current or former partner.
- Intimate partner violence is the greatest health risk factor for women aged 25–44.

CHAPTER FIVE: INDIVIDUALISM, POPULISM AND IDENTITY POLITICS

- An estimated one in six women (1.6 million) aged 18 years and over have experienced violence by a partner since the age of 15.
- Young women (18–24 years) experience significantly higher rates of physical and sexual violence than women in older age groups.
- Approximately one in four women (23% or 2.2 million) have experienced violence by an intimate partner since the age of 15.
- Domestic or family violence against women is the single largest driver of homelessness for women, a common factor in child protection notifications, and results in a police call-out on average once every two minutes across the country.
- More than two-thirds (68%) of mothers who had children in their care when they experienced violence from their previous partner said their children had seen or heard the violence.[89]

What the above discussion of liberalism's excesses demonstrates is that democracy is in serious trouble. When enough citizens take the freedoms that liberal democracy affords as their own individual freedoms, thereby ignoring their responsibility to work also for the freedom of others, democracy is on a slippery slope to authoritarianism where freedoms are granted only at the whim of a dictator. How to move the focus away from hyper-individualism to a more egalitarian, community-based focus is the great challenge of this current historical moment.

The first thing for us to do, as serious thinkers, is to stop panicking and try to understand how democratic societies of today arrived at this point. It is my hope that the discussion of populism to follow will go some way toward achieving that.

---

89   Safe Steps. n.d. 'Family and Domestic Violence Statistics in Australia'. <https://www.safesteps.org.au/statistics/#>.

Populism

First, what is populism? Most dictionaries and encyclopaedias are in agreement with the definition offered by the European Centre for Populism Studies:

> Populism refers to a range of political stances that emphasize the idea of 'the people' and often juxtapose this group against 'the elite' ...
>
> A common framework for interpreting populism is known as the ideational approach: this defines populism as an ideology which presents 'the people' as a morally good force and contrasts them against 'the elite', who are portrayed as corrupt and self-serving.[90]

So, it is a movement of people who believe that they – 'the people'– are virtuous, and who are working together to depose the "corrupt elite" whose governments, legal systems and media are deliberately working against the people.

The populist movement expresses serious concerns about economic inequality, immigration policies that are 'far too generous' and refugees being granted asylum. The movement is inward-focused, which is why Donald Trump's slogan 'Make America Great Again' resonated with so many citizens in the United States, and why populists in other countries were quick to imitate the theme. In Australia, the chant sometimes heard at meetings and rallies, 'freedom, freedom', was often accompanied by calls to 'Make Australia Great Again'.

Populism rejects liberal-democratic values such as equality and diversity, and discriminates against people on the basis of race, religion and ethnic origin. Scientific facts are ridiculed as tools used by the elite against the people, but 'facts' trending on social media are judged to be acceptable. Mainstream media

---

[90] European Centre for Populism Studies, n.d. 'Populism'. <https://www.populismstudies.org/Vocabulary/populism>.

CHAPTER FIVE: INDIVIDUALISM, POPULISM AND IDENTITY POLITICS

is often accused of spreading 'fake news'. The legal system is weakened, too, by populist leaders who choose to ignore the need for fairness. The extra-judicial killings ordered by the former President of the Philippines, Rodrigo Duterte, is a recent example of a populist leader ignoring the need for judicial fairness. President Donald Trump, too, with no regard for fairness, weakened the court system in the United States by appointing as judges only those people who he knew were committed to right-wing politics.

For many of us, the phenomenon we now know as populism, came to our attention as we tried to grapple with the fact that Donald Trump had so much support from so many people in the United States and beyond. How could it be that so many women voted for him and still support him, we asked, after remarks like:

> I'm automatically attracted to beautiful [women]. I just start kissing them. It's like a magnet. Just kiss. I don't even wait ... When you're a star, they let you do it. You can do anything. Grab 'em by the pussy. You can do anything.[91]

And how could it be that so many fundamentalist Christians almost worship at his feet? And African Americans and people from diverse ethnic backgrounds, when he clearly supports white supremacists? And how could educated people support him when so much of what he says is inconsistent, incoherent and puzzling?

Populism did not start with Donald Trump but, in democratic countries, was given permission to break out of its repressed state by Trump's audacity, by his willingness to trample on every tradition that democracies hold dear.

At first, my assessment was that all of those people caught up in the populist movement were acting like teenagers determined to go against everything their parents valued and that they, like

---

91 <https://www.vox.com/2016/10/7/13205842/trump-secret-recording-women>.

teenagers, would 'grow out of it'. I held out hope that everything would settle down and that those who were expressing such strong resentments against society's traditions and systems would once again come to terms with the system as it is and find peace. I feel somewhat embarrassed confessing my original thoughts and feelings because I realise now that, as well as being short on analysis, it was quite arrogant. It was what I *wanted* to have happen rather than the result of any in-depth analysis. What I needed to do was take the time to empathise and try to understand why so many people were so discontented.

After much reading and contemplation, I have reached the conclusion that populism has the capacity to change democratic societies for the better provided that we who are labelled 'elites' – governments, universities, feminists, human rights activists, the wealthy – have the humility to listen rather than condemn.

The first step is truth-seeking. What has caused the populist rebellion against democratic traditions in so many countries? There are three main propositions being raised by social and political analysts that deserve our attention: powerlessness, contempt and humiliation.

Populism as a response to powerlessness

Ulrike Guerot, Professor and Director of the Department for European Policy and the Study of Democracy at Danube University Krems, reminded readers that, a century ago, "populism was the pride of social democracy." Mentioning left-wing leaders such as Jean Jaurés, Léon Blum and Jules Ferry, she said:

> These were men who cared for the people, especially exploited workers; they wanted to improve their lives. Caring was their key word.

CHAPTER FIVE: INDIVIDUALISM, POPULISM AND IDENTITY POLITICS

> Today, nobody seems to care for people. The European losers in today's globalisation, people living, and failing, mostly in devastated rural areas, are mainly left to themselves. If they fail, due to lack of education and life chances, they're told they are living in free societies, where everybody has the potential to succeed.

Populism stems from the fact that "opportunity remains a fiction for many people," she said (Guerot in Keane 2016).

On the same panel, John Keane, Professor of Politics at the University of Sydney, commented:

> Populism is a democratic phenomenon. Mobilised through available democratic freedoms, it's a public protest by millions of people ... who feel annoyed, powerless, no longer 'held' in the arms of society (Keane 2016).

One does have to ask of today's liberal-democracy: Where are the principles of equality, community and free speech? Where is the caring community that attempts to hold everyone in its arms? For ordinary people, democratic principles seem to be principles from the past because the imbalance of power is obvious to everyone. Without a doubt, power lies with multinational companies, big business and the business lobby and, for everyone else, there are degrees of powerlessness. The lobbying of governments by the business lobby is itself big business, and politicians listen enthusiastically to all that the lobbyists have to say in a desperate attempt to curry favour with those who have the power to generate jobs as well as wealth for the nation. Meanwhile, it is proving more and more difficult for ordinary people to get a hearing from politicians. A person may make an appointment with their local member of parliament to discuss an important issue but, when the time comes, it is often the admin officer or other assistant who shows up for the interview – with the promise that he or she will pass the information on to the local member. Is it any wonder that citizens give up trying to be heard and live with the feeling that nobody with any power to make changes can be bothered listening?

For many, social media is where they find others who will listen and take their concerns seriously. There they find people who feel the same kind of disenchantment because they, too, feel disenfranchised. Joining together with others who empathise with them makes them feel less powerless, indeed, more powerful. It is at that point that many feel drawn to populist political leaders who are highly critical of the system and its traditions. Such leaders give the impression that they understand the powerlessness people feel and paint a picture of a much more inclusive future. The powerlessness that many people feel today must be addressed if democracy is to be saved.

Populism as a response to contempt

In an essay, 'Uncivil Wars: How Contempt is Corroding Democracy', journalists Waleed Aly and Scott Stephens make the point that democracy can survive "anger, resentment, envy, vengefulness [and] shame" but it cannot survive contempt. "[C]ontempt has been almost universally condemned as the kind of moral emotion from which nothing good can come" (Aly and Stephens 2022, p. 11).

The authors make a simple comparison:

> Democracy is about cultivating a common life even in the presence of serious disagreement. Contempt is about having no life in common at all (p. 7).

Aly and Stephens begin by reminding readers of Hillary Clinton's expression of contempt during her campaign to become America's first woman president. On 9 September 2016, she gave a campaign speech which election analysts mark as the moment that thousands of undecided voters turned against her and made up their minds to vote for Donald Trump:

CHAPTER FIVE: INDIVIDUALISM, POPULISM AND IDENTITY POLITICS

> You know, to just be grossly generalistic, you could put half of Trump's supporters into what I call a basket of deplorables, she said, to laughter from the audience. Right? They're racist, sexist, homophobic, xenophobic, Islamophobic – you name it. And unfortunately, there are people like that ... Now some of those folks – they are irredeemable ... (p. 3).

Did Hillary Clinton really believe that writing off millions of American citizens as 'deplorables' and 'irredeemable' was going to be good for democracy and her party? The utter contempt expressed in those words did not go unnoticed by those targeted. Not only did they move away from Clinton and toward Trump but, also, away from democracy to populism.

It is too easy to write off those one disagrees with, to hold them in contempt and refuse to make room for the possibility of finding at least some common ground. As Aly and Stephens say of contempt in general: "we see no future with our political opponents because we feel we have nothing to learn from them." It's obvious in the way we characterise each other, they point out:

> ... it's not that our opponents are partial, uninformed, mistaken, unwise, naïve ... Instead, we tell ourselves, and anyone else who will listen, that our opponents are sub-rational, bigoted, toxic, dangerous, malignant, wilfully ignorant, cynically self-interested, fundamentally dishonest – in a word, inferior in every way that matters – and hence incapable of good-faith disagreement (2022, p. 52).

Contempt attacks the very essence of a person. It is no wonder, then, that people who feel judged by 'elites' (whether it is true or not), find solace and affirmation with others who express the feeling that they, too, are held in contempt. Populism provides the sense of belonging that they are craving, the sense of belonging that democracy promises but is failing to deliver.

Populism as a response to humiliation

When Michael Sandel, Professor of Government Theory at Harvard Law School asked: "What sense can we make of our current political moment?" he followed that up with a further question: "Is it possible to imagine a politics that could respond to the anxieties and the frustrations that are roiling democratic politics around the world?"

In his address to the Royal Society for the Encouragement of Arts, Manufactures and Commerce in 2018 (and repeated on ABC Radio National's *Big Ideas* in 2020), Sandel argues that "mainstream political parties fail to understand the social alienation that drives people to embrace populist politics." For four decades, globalisation has been enthusiastically carried out by both conservative and centre-left political parties by embracing what Sandel calls a neoliberal/technocratic approach to government. The dominant belief was that the market was the way to achieve the public good, as if it were possible to outsource moral and political judgements to markets, or to experts and technocrats. "This approach to public discourse," he says, "has created an empty, impoverished public discourse, a vacuum of public meaning." It has also brought a growing inequality and has given rise to a politics of humiliation.

The neoliberal/technocratic approach that preaches "you can make it if you try" creates winners and losers, and encourages the impression that those who have 'made it' have done so on their own merit. One problem with meritocracy is that it allows those who make it because of their talents to feel that they *deserve* to be winners, as if being blessed with talents is their own doing. Similarly, it allows those who have had the privilege of higher education to feel superior to those who, perhaps because of their family's financial constraints, have not. Writing about the effects

CHAPTER FIVE: INDIVIDUALISM, POPULISM AND IDENTITY POLITICS

of meritocracy on those who are seen to be 'losers' in the system, Sandel says:

> For those who feel aggrieved by the tyranny of merit, the problem is not only economic disadvantage but the loss of social esteem. The grievance is not only about unfairness. It is also about humiliation.[92]

This humiliation felt by so many people has prompted the populist backlash evident today in democratic countries around the world, to the point that democracy itself is being threatened in a way that has never been evident before. In concluding his address, Sandel says:

> To reinvigorate democratic politics, we need to find our way to a morally more robust public discourse, one that takes seriously the corrosive effect of meritocratic striving and the social bonds that constitute our common life. Disentangling the intolerant aspects of populist protest from its legitimate grievances is no easy matter, but it is important to try. Understanding these grievances and creating a politics that can respond to them is the most pressing political challenge of our time.[93]

It does seem to be true that many citizens of democratic countries around the world are suffering because of powerlessness, contempt and/or humiliation and that that is fuelling the populist movement. If democracy is to survive, it is therefore imperative that both 'the people' and 'the elite' find ways to work with goodwill to find common ground rather than continuing to cancel each other. In other words, individualism and tribalism must give way to a sense of shared community.

---

92   Michael Sandel, 12 March 2020, 'Overcoming Division with the Politics of Hope', *ABC Big Ideas*. <https://www.abc.net.au/radionational/programs/bigideas/overcoming-division-with-the-politics-of-hope/12030496>.
93   ibid.

Identity politics

The most obvious example of the excesses of liberalism in recent decades is today's version of 'identity politics'. While a very different phenomenon from populism, it is nonetheless a product of today's hyper-individualism.

What is identity politics? According to the *Stanford Encyclopedia of Philosophy*, the phrase signifies "a wide range of political activity and theorizing founded in the shared experiences of injustice of members of certain social groups."[94] By this definition, the liberation movements of the 1960s and 1970s are examples of identity politics and, while the term 'identity politics' was coined by the Combahee River Collective (an African-American lesbian feminist organisation) in Boston in 1977,[95] it was not a term that was commonly used. Women, racial minorities, lesbians and gay men all rose up, spoke out and demanded recognition, respect and an equal share of power. While there was less than a wholehearted response from the white middle-class men in power, those involved in the movements were determined to make an impact and bring about systemic change.

Women, in particular, began analysing and writing about the oppression of women in patriarchy's systems, writing about their own and other women's experiences of violence and intimidation at the hands of men, of lost opportunities due to their invisibility in the workplace, lost history, sexual exploitation and disempowerment. Feminists were determined to be heard and, for a time, a better future for women seemed to be in sight.

---

94 *Stanford Encyclopedia of Philosophy*. n.d. 'Identity Politics'. <https://plato.stanford.edu/entries/identity-politics/>.
95 <https://www.theguardian.com/commentisfree/2020/feb/10/identity-politics-bernie-sanders-endorsement>.

CHAPTER FIVE: INDIVIDUALISM, POPULISM AND IDENTITY POLITICS

Then came the watering down of feminism's radical demands, and it was then that the term 'identity politics' began to be used to indicate individual empowerment. Instead of focusing on changing an oppressive patriarchal system, liberal feminists argued that more would be achieved if the movement worked *with* men instead of the angry confrontations that characterised the early years of Second Wave feminism. Such watering-down brought with it the appearance of change but, as radicals expected, very little actual change. Nancy Fraser, philosopher, feminist, Professor of Political and Social Science at the New School for Social Research in New York City, expressed her concern in a piece in *The Guardian* in 2013, 'How feminism became capitalism's handmaiden – and how to reclaim it'. She said:

> As a feminist, I've always assumed that by fighting to emancipate women I was building a better world – more egalitarian, just and free. But lately I've begun to worry that ideals pioneered by feminists are serving quite different ends. I worry, specifically, that our critique of sexism is now supplying the justification for new forms of inequality and exploitation.

Focusing particularly on neoliberalism, Fraser went on to say:

> ... I fear that the movement for women's liberation has become entangled in a dangerous liaison with neoliberal efforts to build a free-market society. That would explain how it came to pass that feminist ideas that once formed part of a radical worldview are increasingly expressed in individualist terms.[96]

The big change from the politics of the 1970s liberation movements to the identity politics of today is just that – from a push for systemic change inspired by a 'radical worldview' to a focus on

---

96 Nancy Fraser, 14 October 2013, 'How Feminism Became Capitalism's Handmaiden and How to Reclaim It', *The Guardian*. <https://www.theguardian.com/commentisfree/2013/oct/14/feminism-capitalist-handmaiden-neoliberal?CMP=Share_iOSApp_Other>.

the 'individual'. With the help of liberal feminists, neoliberalism co-opted the feminist idea of empowerment for women and turned the "dream of women's emancipation" into a desire for individual success in the form of "capital accumulation," Fraser said.[97]

Meagan Tyler, in an opinion piece 'Can feminism be saved from identity politics?' (2021), also emphasises neoliberalism's contribution to the trend toward the individualising of feminism and feminist aims:

> Like so much political debate that has passed through the prism of neoliberalism – and we must appreciate the importance of neoliberalism to this trend – 'identity' has moved from a politically and sociologically informed understanding of power and social categories, to a more psychologised, individual understanding of a freely-chosen sense of self. This has had serious consequences for feminist activism, and even for how feminism itself is conceptualised.[98]

Instead of a radical social movement, she says, feminism has become in the minds of many today a personal lifestyle choice, and feminist activism is focused on making life better for individual women within an unchanged system.

How does the move into identity politics undermine the aims of feminist activism as Fraser and Tyler insist? It does so by creating a politics based on hyper-individualism. Instead of focusing on the underlying, systemic oppression of certain groups in society, and confronting today's patriarchal, capitalist system with a view to changing it, many activists today seem content to argue for one group of people while seeking to silence others.

---

97 ibid.
98 Meagan Tyler, 8 March 2021, 'Can Feminism Be Saved from Identity Politics?' *ABC Religion & Ethics*. <https://www.abc.net.au/religion/can-feminism-be-saved-from-identity- politics/11646084>.

CHAPTER FIVE: INDIVIDUALISM, POPULISM AND IDENTITY POLITICS

To illustrate the way identity politics pits group against group, I will focus here on the identity group that has aggressively forced itself on to centre stage in recent times, i.e., transgender-identified people. While it is mainly those on the left of politics, including so-called 'progressive' governments, liberal human rights defenders and liberal feminists, who are agitating with and on behalf of the trans lobby (those, incidentally, who see themselves as staunch defenders of liberal democracy), it must be said that the attitudes and tactics of the trans lobby are distinctly anti-liberal and anti-democratic.

Here I will highlight just four of the many ways that this occurs.

1. While defenders of liberal democracy respect history and tradition, *trans activists seek to change history by erasing the record of their birth* and replacing historical facts with new, constructed 'facts'. This kind of pretence not only threatens to render the study of history redundant, it also has the potential to destabilise societies. A shared understanding of history has always provided a degree of stability in any society and moving into a situation that questions the trustworthiness of the facts of history will surely have a negative effect on that stability.

   Many so-called progressive governments have bowed to the demands of the trans lobby and introduced self-identification laws that allow for the changing of a person's sex on her or his birth certificate. Since self-deceit is known to be psychologically damaging and a recipe for a life of depression, one wonders why governments are so ready to collude with such a pretence, unless it is that they will do anything to escape the wrath of such aggressive proponents of identity politics.

2. While democracy emphasises the need for societies to be built on shared truths, trans activists *suspend truth in their insistence on language change* to accommodate their chosen identity. Regardless of the fact that cultures around the world have always identified men and women with the pronouns 'he' and 'she' and most of the world's population continues to be satisfied with those descriptors, the trans lobby has decreed that sex-identifying pronouns be replaced by non-sex-identifying ones like 'they'. Sadly, many governments, universities, courts and other 'woke' institutions support the trans decree and some employees have even lost their jobs over 'misnaming' someone, that is, using the wrong pronoun.

Also, 'mother' is set to be made redundant and replaced by 'birthing parent' regardless of protests by midwives' associations, nursing bodies, medical associations and, of course, mothers themselves. The trans rationale 'men give birth too' is surely a classic example of the suspension of truth. The male body has not been designed to experience pregnancy or to give birth. When it appears that a man has given birth, the truth is that it is a woman identifying as a man who has given birth – and she is able to perform that function because, biologically, she is a woman.

A similar suspension of truth occurs in the area of female genital mutilation (FGM). Activists against FGM report that their work in supporting survivors and raising awareness in the community of the violence perpetrated against girls through the practice of FGM has now run into trouble. They are harassed and trolled by trans activists and their supporters for using the term *female* genital mutilation and for identifying girls and women as victims/survivors. As with the claim that men can give birth, I say again that the genital mutilation referred to in the trans community by those living as men and boys occurred when they were girls. Hence, it is still female genital mutilation.

The potential for the spread of disinformation, indeed lies, around the insistence on changing pronouns and language in general is enormous.

3. While the sharing of ideas, acceptance of opposing views and the will to compromise are central principles of liberal democracy, *most trans activists refuse to consider alternative opinions.* They require 100% agreement and anyone who voices a different view on any of their issues is shut up, trolled, abused, threatened and cancelled. They will brook no argument or entertain any suggestions for compromise.

4. The democratic focus on equality and fairness is clearly absent when trans activists *continue to place trans issues above the issues of all other oppressed groups.* In the ever-evolving acronym LGBTQIA+, all other initials are subject to the T. Indeed, some lesbians, gay men and bisexuals have made it known that, for that very reason, they have withdrawn from the acronym. LGB groups have formed with the aim of having their own issues come out from under the domination of the T, so that they can once again be heard by the wider society. Similarly, the lesbian group 'Get the L Out' makes a point of distancing itself from the LGBT group. Their protest is against what they see as the erasure of lesbians and the influence of gender identity politics. The transgender lobby shows little interest in working together with other oppressed groups in an equal and fair way.

Of particular concern is their deliberate refusal to consider the oppression that women experience on a daily basis, the violence, the fear, the struggle to be heard, the invisibility. Trans people and their many supporters seemingly have no interest in how their demands are affecting adult human females: women who have been female since birth. Women's safety is to be sacrificed in order that transwomen may feel 'safe'. Every social group, every sporting activity, every toilet and changing room, every prison, all spaces that historically were kept separate for a variety of reasons including women's fear of men's violence, are now to be open to men. As extraordinary as it may be, many of them will be genitally-intact men, and all will be men who have grown up with the lessons of aggression that society teaches men and boys.

If today's identity politics is a destructive force as I am asserting, how is it that so many academics, feminists, politicians and community leaders have bought into it so wholeheartedly?

One reason could be that the public shaming of anyone who dares speak out against any of the prominent identity groups calling for attention to their rights is too much to bear. Choosing to stay under the radar by passively assenting to the demands of aggressive minority groups allows a person or an institution to get on with their work without the drama of being 'outed' and called on to explain.

Another reason could be that they have misunderstood or misinterpreted the concept of 'intersectionality', a term coined by Kimberlé Crenshaw in the late 1980s. Crenshaw drew attention to the fact that the oppression experienced by black women is different from that experienced by white women, due to the fact that black women are disempowered on two fronts: being a woman and being black. For a black woman with a disability, the disempowerment is threefold ... and so on. Her point was that it is the *intersection* of areas of discrimination *within a person* that needs to be addressed. However, many liberal feminists and human rights activists today are using the concept of 'intersectionality' to justify their support for individual issues where there is no actual intersection. As Crenshaw herself pointed out in an interview at the Columbia Law School in 2017,

CHAPTER FIVE: INDIVIDUALISM, POPULISM AND IDENTITY POLITICS

many people are using the term today in a way that is antithetical to its original meaning:

> Intersectionality is a lens through which you can see where power comes and collides, where it interlocks and intersects. It's not simply that there's a race problem here, a gender problem here, and a class or LGBTQ problem there.[99]

The co-opting of intersectionality to support today's individualised version of identity politics makes no sense.

To sum up, the excesses of liberalism, the distressing spectacle of populism and the aggressive nature of today's identity politics all demonstrate the fact that individualism is anti-democratic. It goes against the principles of democracy that invite citizens to participate in government by scrutinising decisions made on their behalf and giving feedback to elected politicians. Instead of thinking of society as a mass of individuals freely making their own decisions and doing their own thing, citizens are encouraged to see themselves as part of a collective, and fulfil their responsibility to challenge society's systems and work together with others to bring about the changes needed.

◇◇◇

One question remains: What is the role that feminist theory and practice will play in ensuring the survival of democracy? As I will argue in Chapter Six, a proven commitment to truth together with unwavering courage in speaking truth to power stand radical feminists in good stead to take a leading role in efforts to save and reinvigorate democracy.

---

99 Kimberlé Crenshaw, 8 June 2017, 'Kimberlé Crenshaw on Intersectionality, More Than Two Decades Later', Columbia Law School. <https://www.law.columbia.edu/news/archive/kimberle-crenshaw-intersectionality-more-two-decades-later>.

CHAPTER SIX

Leading the Way

In the quest to save democracy from the destructive behaviour currently eating away at it from the inside, feminism can shine a light on the path to a new relationship with truth. It will not be a liberal/mainstream feminism, operating at a superficial level and open to saying 'yes' to everything in the name of equality. It will not be a conservative feminism, poised to say 'no' to anything and everything that could disrupt the status quo. It will be a *radical* feminism, uncompromised and uncompromising, prepared to go beneath the surface and analyse issues in depth in order to discover the truth in every situation before taking a stand and moving forward.

This chapter is written with hope and positivity, and takes its place in a long line of feminist predictions and hopes about the future influence of feminism. In the Introduction, I began by pointing to some of those imagined futures and, here, I add two more.

Germaine Greer, for example, wrote about the future in the final page of her 1999 book *The Whole Woman*, and her predictions are thought-provoking and powerful:

> The second wave of feminism, rather than having crashed on to the shore, is still far out to sea, slowly and inexorably gathering momentum. None of us who are alive today will witness more than the first rumbles of the coming social upheaval. Middle-class western women have the privilege of serving the longest

revolution, not of directing it. The ideological battles that feminist theorists are engaged in are necessary but they are preliminary to the emergence of female power, which will not flow decorously out from the universities or from the consumerist women's press. Female power will rush upon us in the person of women who have nothing to lose, having lost everything already.

She continues with some poignant examples:

It could surge up in China where so many women divorced for bearing girl children are living and working together, or in Thailand where prostitution and AIDS are destroying a generation, in Iran or anywhere else where women are on a collision course with Islamic fundamentalism, or anywhere the famished labourer sees luxury foods for the western market grown on the land which used to provide for her and her children.

Greer concludes with a warning to women from affluent countries:

And the women of the rich world had better hope that when female energy ignites they do not find themselves on the wrong side (Greer 1999, p. 330).

Susan Hawthorne, after testifying in the final pages of *Vortex: The Crisis of Patriarchy*, to the fact that "the advent of feminism changed my life," then expresses her hopes for the future. While different in tenor from the future predictions of Germaine Greer, her expressions of hope are just as powerful:

My hope for the future is that mass movements can recreate the world in new ways. My hope is for a world enlivened by meaningful relationship, with freedom from violence in all its forms including epistemic violence, for decolonisation and recognition that the colonised have never ceded their lands and cultures. I hope for a world in which women can walk the streets without fear at any time of the day; that men will call out members of the male sex when they threaten women in any way; that children grow up to be the adults they want to be without the strictures of gender.

She continues in a manner that is all-inclusive and inspiring:

> I hope that the world will be a friendlier place for those with disabilities and a recognition that disability is something that occurs in most living beings at some time in our lives. My hope is that the richness of many cultures and languages can become a way of life and that the learning of more than one language becomes the norm, alongside access to creative expression through the arts. I also hope that many readers' voices will add to these small hopes and bring their own cultural depth, texture and knowledge to this currently fragile world (Hawthorne 2020, pp. 255–56).

Here, I am adding my own voice to the variety of predictions about the future influence of feminism by saying: We will lead the way. Feminism will offer a way out of the darkness and into the light where truth is once again a central feature of a healthy democracy.

How will that happen? How will we begin to effect such a transformation?

First, we will continue to *uncover and describe the root causes of the weakening of democracy*, demonstrating that truth-telling is imperative. Second, we will work at *changing narratives* to reflect a more truthful, though still positive, picture of everyday life. Third, we will continue to be involved in *actions across all areas* where change to the status quo is deemed necessary. And fourth, we will identify allies in the struggle and *work together with like-minded others* on this forward-moving journey.

Uncovering root causes

A major theme throughout this book has been this: A lack of respect for truth will eventually destroy democracy. Working to uncover root causes is an exercise in searching for the truth and, then, having the courage to reveal that truth. Here, I must issue a warning however. Positing a lack of respect for truth as a root cause of anything can be far too simple because the cause of something is often the effect of something deeper.

Consequently, a search for 'the' root cause can be never-ending and all-consuming. As soon as one remarks that democracy is being destroyed by a careless handling of the truth, it could be asked: what is causing such a careless attitude toward the truth? The answer then may focus on a loss of integrity or a general loss of the need for authenticity. This may then be followed by a further question: but what is the root cause of such loss of integrity and loss of the need for authenticity. And so on.

As feminists shining a light on the path ahead, it is important that we avoid being rendered impotent by the need always to dig deeper. We must be satisfied with a 'cause' that is supported by personal testimonies and scientific facts, and work to uncover and describe that cause as fully as possible before eventually going deeper.

Chapters One and Two of this book are full of examples of feminists and other women working to uncover root causes of anti-democratic attitudes and practices relating to women. Courageous women have uncovered and expressed the truth about their own and other women's experiences of men's violence in the home, on the street and in work and social situations. Also, feminist researchers have analysed at depth and uncovered the truth about such practices as prostitution, pornography, surrogacy, rape, harassment and sexual abuse of children. The root cause of the intractable statistics of men's violation, domination and demeaning of women, according to feminist researchers, is the unequal power relations between men and women, in other words, patriarchy's support of men's 'right' to exercise power over women.

CHAPTER SIX: LEADING THE WAY

The concept of power has been the subject of much feminist analysis from the early years of Second Wave feminism right up to today. Important research has revealed that men's need to have power over others is the root cause, not only of their violent behaviour toward women but, also, of their use of violence more generally.

The wars waged by Russia against Ukraine and between Hamas and Israel are prime examples of the extent to which patriarchal governments and terrorist groups are prepared to go to demonstrate their power. The destruction of human life, the bombing of hospitals, the kidnapping of the enemy's children, the denying of safe passage out of war zones for innocent civilians are all, it seems, 'acceptable' in the pursuit of power.

It must be said that seeking to have power over others for its own sake is antithetical to the principles of democracy, whether it be physical power or power that comes from the pursuit of wealth and influence.

Focusing on the need for truth, I demonstrated in Chapters Three, Four and Five of this book, that a careless handling of the truth by patriarchy's leaders is often for the purpose of holding on to power and/or to maintain wealth and influence. Politicians, business leaders and others in positions of power have much invested in keeping patriarchal, dominant-culture structures in place, and they can do so almost by stealth. The aim, it seems, is to keep citizens believing that democratic principles are being adhered to while, at the same time, operating in secret to keep their power relationships alive by privileging the needs of a few.

Our ethical task is to put fear aside, analyse root causes and lead the way in exposing lies, illegal practices and other antidemocratic behaviours. While uncovering and revealing the truth takes courage, as feminists and other whistle-blowers through the ages will testify, it is imperative that truth be at the centre if democracy is to remain strong.

Changing narratives

Uncovering and revealing root causes is an ongoing task. So also is the task of seeking to understand the narratives that influence people's attitudes and behaviour and, where necessary, working to change them. There are national narratives, and there are also everyday narratives alive in the community.

First, I will point to examples of national narratives. Every nation has narratives about itself. A narrative in the United States might be something like this: "We are a decent people, strong, caring, God-fearing upholders of human rights." This narrative, given the ruthlessness with which the United States deals with other nations at times, the revenge mentality since the 9/11 terrorist attacks, the refusal to take away people's right to bear arms in the face of so much human tragedy, surely is in need of a rethink.

Australia, too, has certain narratives that are in need of change. Acknowledging its convict beginnings, white Australia proudly believes: "We're a larrikin mob – with a big heart." However, the resounding defeat of the 2023 referendum asking Australian citizens to agree to a small change in the constitution to give Aboriginal and Torres Strait Islander peoples a voice as the first people, puts a lie to the 'big heart' narrative. Another example is that mentioned in Chapter Three regarding Australia's on-going detention of asylum-seekers, imprisoned (some for more than ten years) for no greater 'crime' than that of travelling by boat in search of a better life. A big heart – except, it seems, in relation to Indigenous people, refugees, women, people with disabilities, those living in poverty, and others. Another popular Australian narrative, very close in meaning to the one above, is: "We believe in a fair go for all."

Then, there is the narrative: "We are a peace-loving nation," except for the fact that whenever the United States calls on

CHAPTER SIX: LEADING THE WAY

its allies to support one of its wars, regardless of how unjust a particular war may be judged to be by large numbers of Australian citizens (Vietnam or Iraq, for example), we as a nation do not hesitate in offering up the lives of our young men and women to fight and, if need be, to die in support of America's cause.

One of the important tasks for feminists as we seek to lead the way into a future where truth is once again a central part of democracy is to encourage truth-telling in relation to the narratives one's nation rests on. Many of the old narratives may need to be replaced by new, more up-to-date, more truthful ones, but that does not mean it has to be a negative exercise. Narratives expressing hope, for example, will have the positive effect of encouraging citizens to look to the future with confidence.

In addition to national narratives, there are also everyday narratives that need our attention as feminists who seek to lead the way in developing a better understanding of democracy. Some that I focused on earlier in this book are among those everyday narratives in need of change.

Democracy champions the rights of the individual over all else must be changed to ***Democracy is a story of the individual within a collective, and focuses on the rights and responsibilities of the individual as a member of a society.***

As a democracy, we believe in equality must be changed to ***As a democracy, we are committed to equity and fairness.***

Democracy gives me the right to unlimited free speech must be changed to ***Democracy champions fair speech, that is, free speech that does no harm, and is equally available to all.***

Democracy calls for unconditional, unquestioning acceptance of the identity another person has chosen must be changed to ***Democracy calls for acceptance based on truth.***

The capitalist narrative *Everyone can be a winner if they try hard enough* must be changed to reflect the reality of family circumstances, intellectual abilities and roadblocks that may exist. The new narrative should read: *Democracy values cooperative interactions over competitiveness, and encourages a focus on the social good.*

By working to change the narratives of one's nation as well as everyday narratives that diminish community life, feminists will be helping to enrich individual lives and create societies based on truth.

It must be said, however, that changing narratives is not easy. When one considers that governments often work hard to create false narratives for the purpose of ensuring their own political longevity, it must be understood that they and the people who have bought into their false narratives, will strongly resist change. So, I offer this warning: Changing narratives ought only to be attempted if it can be done without destroying people's hopes and only if those narratives can be replaced by something better. *Truth* must be promoted as a more worthwhile alternative.

Why is a focus on changing narratives necessary? Because the stories citizens believe about themselves and their nation, that is, the narratives people live by, influence attitudes and behaviour. It follows, therefore, that when false narratives are changed, it is likely that there will also be changes in attitudes and behaviour.

If this reads like an exercise in the re-education of whole societies, the truth is, it is. But no more than the re-education attempted by all social movements, protest movements, public rallies, demonstrations and marches. All such social action aims unashamedly at influencing attitudes and behaviour. In contrast to a protest march which is organised as a one-off event for maximum effect, however, the task of changing narratives as I'm referring to it here, is a long-term project that will require patience and a generally positive attitude toward other people and their ability – and willingness – to change.

CHAPTER SIX: LEADING THE WAY

Action across all areas

The world today is different from the way it was when the Women's Liberation Movement burst on to the global stage in the 1960s but, in significant ways, it is still the same. Regardless of decades of passionate activism on the part of feminists and others, the industries around prostitution, trafficking, pornography and surrogacy still exist and are in fact growing; statistics of women violated, mutilated and murdered by men show no change, except to increase; and women are still blamed for men's violent behaviour. As the world becomes more conservative, religious and political fundamentalism continue to strip women of their basic rights.

Wherever there is a need, feminists are working across all areas to respond, first, by exposing government neglect and, then, by working with a number of diverse groups to provide practical help to women and men affected by homelessness, poverty, Indigenous disadvantage, access to health services, discrimination against those with disabilities, and so on.

Calling out police brutality, holding the law to account when injustices are evident in the courts, protesting against the holding of children in police watch houses, speaking up for the rights of women held in prison on remand for lengthy periods – all of these are sites of activism for feminists.

Feminists are on the front line, too, of environmental activism, including protests around lack of climate action on the part of governments and businesses. In government, in the media, in foreign policy, feminists are adding their voices in important ways.

In western countries, where women have fought hard to have the same access to speech as men, there is a growing concern about the fact that women now are being silenced in favour of the free speech rights of the transgender community. Feminists along with all women and men who try to protest against the false identification of men as women find that they are being shut up and shut out of any possibility of dialogue. Feminists continue fighting this crucial battle for free speech.

There are many other areas where feminists are at the forefront of battles fought to ensure the democratic rights of women and men, but the above will suffice to make the point that feminists need to keep on working across all areas into the future. More expansive work needs to be done around social media and, in the very near future, we will see more feminists tackling the difficult phenomenon of AI. One thing we can be assured of is that, as in the past, feminists of the future will be everywhere, watching, commenting, protesting and working for change.

Moving forward together

Moving forward requires four things, three of which have already been discussed: an ongoing commitment to truth-telling about root causes; careful attention to the narratives that guide people's lives; and a continued commitment to activism across all areas. The fourth is that of identifying allies in the struggle.

The word 'together' in the heading 'Moving forward together' is crucial due to the fact that moving forward in the quest to save democracy from extinction would be extremely difficult without a willingness on the part of all social justice defenders, including radical feminists, to work together with like-minded others. Identifying allies is not something that comes easily to radical feminists, given that the legitimacy of our theories is often questioned, but experience has shown that it is possible to work with others without compromising one's own ethics and values, particularly when decisions are made to work on an issue-by-issue basis. For example, liberal feminists are allies in the fight against men's violence against women, but are poles apart from radical feminists on issues involving men's sex rights or the invading of women's spaces by men who claim to be women. On those issues, many radical feminists work comfortably with more conservative women and some men.

Acknowledging the need to continue working across all areas to ensure that democratic values survive and thrive, the search for like-minded others will be more important than ever for the journey ahead. While it will not be possible here to cover all areas, I will mention just a few to demonstrate the kind of partnerships that will bring positive results.

For allies in the fight to preserve the democratic values of *transparency, integrity and truth*, many of the politicians currently serving in the Australian parliament as independents, those, that is, who reveal a particularly enlightened mindset, are allies. Unencumbered by the need to think and speak in unison with a particular political party, some are practised in the art of holding governments and business leaders to account. Some journalists, too, are allies in our quest to keep governments accountable.

In matters relating to *climate change and other environmental issues*, climate activists of all ages are natural allies, as are members of the Greens political party. It should be noted, however, that some of the policies of the Australian Greens differ markedly from those of radical feminists but, on environmental issues, we are allies.

To uphold the values of *diversity, equity and inclusiveness* requires allies from the Indigenous community, activists and elders who have on-going, first-hand experience of speaking out against discrimination and racial abuse. Also, workers from the non-government sector who have their finger on the pulse in relation to multicultural communities, people with disabilities, the homeless, the unemployed and those who live in poverty are important and necessary allies.

A glimpse into a future that has already begun

In conclusion, I repeat this point: It seems almost too simple to say that the fate of democracy depends on people's courage to tell the truth – but that is what it is about.

In every wave of feminism, indeed, in every generation, there are radical women who exhibit amazing courage by uncovering root causes of problems that beset the lives of women and men. Those courageous women write, mobilise, protest and demand change. Second Wave feminism that had its beginnings in the 1960s has been a force to be reckoned with, and it is not over yet. The best is yet to come. As Sheila Jeffreys remarked in the Introduction to her autobiography *Trigger Warning: My Lesbian Feminist Life*:

> I am in the very fortunate position of having been able to contribute to two waves of feminism: the WLM and the new wave that is taking place now (Jeffreys 2020, p. 1).

I agree that what we see occurring right now is a new wave of feminist activism. Indeed, as I read it, it could more correctly be called the next phase of the Women's Liberation Movement or, as it is referred to now, Second Wave feminism, because it is unmistakably radical. It is not presented as a lifestyle choice for liberal thinkers nor is it postmodernism dressed up as third or fourth or fifth wave in an attempt to co-opt serious feminist scholarship. It is a movement determined to expose the misogyny of patriarchy and create a better world – a world that will benefit both women and men.

CHAPTER SIX: LEADING THE WAY

I finish with a glimpse into a future that has already begun, a future focused on a demand for truth. Of all the work being carried out currently by radical feminist thinkers, there are two areas that stand out above the rest, mainly due to the media attention they attract. One is transgender truth and lies, and the other is sex-based crimes against women.

Transgender truth and lies

At a time in history when most academics, politicians and community leaders prefer to stay silent on matters of gender for fear of being 'cancelled' by the transgender lobby, radical feminists are fearless. Their aim is not to discriminate against anyone unfairly but, rather, to insist on telling the truth about people's sex; and to point out when and why sex matters. I mention just two of the many younger feminists who are making their voices heard on this topic today.

Holly Lawford-Smith, Associate Professor in Political Philosophy at the University of Melbourne and author of *Gender-Critical Feminism* (Lawford-Smith 2022) and *Sex Matters: Essays in Gender-Critical Philosophy* (Lawford-Smith 2023), is one academic who is committed to continuing her philosophical analysis in this area. Lawford-Smith stands proudly in the tradition of older feminists like Janice G. Raymond, Germaine Greer, Sheila Jeffreys and many others.

Kajsa Ekis Ekman, Swedish feminist, Marxist and author of several works, including *On the Meaning of Sex: Thoughts about the New Definition of Woman*, rails against the transgender lobby's determination to make women invisible by insisting on gender-neutral language. She writes:

> Without the word woman, it is difficult to talk about women's condition. Without the word woman, it is impossible to understand the oppression of women. And removing the word

woman does not rid us of woman's oppression. Without the word woman, it is difficult for a women's movement to exist (Ekman 2023, p. 311).

Sex-based crimes against women

Sex-based crime is the other area in which younger generations of feminists are passionately involved in the search for truth and justice. In the wake of the #MeToo movement, women's anger persists and feminists are determined to uncover the extent and severity of men's physical and sexual violence against women, to reveal the law's extreme bias against women in matters of rape and sexual assault, to insist on the need for consent and to make known the negative effects of pornography. That we are witnessing a twenty-first century phase of Second Wave feminism is made obvious by the fact that today's younger feminist writers do not hesitate in referencing the work of earlier Second Wave feminists: Germaine Greer, Andrea Dworkin, Catharine MacKinnon, bell hooks, Susan Brownmiller, Gail Dines, Ellen Pence, Judy Atkinson, Liz Kelly and more.

Here I will mention the work of four of the many younger feminists who are having an impact in this area, and then conclude this section by drawing attention to an exciting international feminist initiative: The Declaration on Women's Sex Based Rights.

Jess Hill, Australian investigative journalist and author, is one of the women involved in serious analysis in this current new phase of Second Wave feminism. She was awarded the Stella Prize for her ground-breaking work on coercive violence, titled *See What You Made Me Do: Power, Control and Domestic Abuse* (Hill 2019). This was followed by a three-part documentary series of the same name produced for television in 2021. Also in 2021, she wrote for the Quarterly Essay *The Reckoning – How #MeToo is Changing Australia* (Hill 2021). She then produced a

CHAPTER SIX: LEADING THE WAY

second documentary series, *Asking For It*, which aired on SBS television in 2023.

As quoted earlier, Jess Hill strongly recommends asking men focused questions like: "What will it take for your kind to stop coercing, harassing, raping, and killing women?" Also, to those in power: "What will it take for you to stop protecting the men who perpetrate this?" (Hill 2021, p. 3). These are questions that go to the very root of the problem of sex-based crimes against women.

Jennifer Robinson, Australian human rights lawyer and barrister with Doughty Street Chambers in London, and Keina Yoshida, international human rights lawyer and visiting fellow for the Centre for Women, Peace and Security at the London School of Economics, are the authors of *How Many More Women? Exposing How the Law Silences Women* (2022). In this powerful book, they too ask radical questions that demand answers:

> HOW MANY MORE WOMEN
> have to be raped or abused before we act?
> need to accuse him before we believe her?
> will be failed by the criminal justice system?
> need to say something before we do something?
> will be sued for defamation for speaking out?
> will be contracted to silence?
> (Robinson and Yoshida 2022, back cover).

Chanel Contos, representing a younger generation than those mentioned above, studied and taught at the University of New South Wales, before being granted a Masters Degree in Education, Gender and International Development at University College London. She is the founder of the Teach Us Consent campaign in Australia and Chair of the Global Institute for Women's Leadership's Global Youth Advisory Committee. Her 2023 book *Consent Laid Bare: Sex, Entitlement & the Distortion of Desire* (Contos 2023) illustrates in a powerful way the difficulties women and men of her generation have in negotiating relationships. Hers is an analysis that goes right to the root of the problem, and she is not afraid to name patriarchy, pornography, violence, rape culture and lack of accountability as issues in dire need of change.

Women's Declaration International (WDI) is a recent movement, powered by a "group of volunteer women from across the globe dedicated to protecting women's sex-based rights." The Declaration on Women's Sex Based Rights developed by the group begins with nine articles:

- Article 1: Reaffirming that the rights of women are based upon the category of sex
- Article 2: Reaffirming the nature of motherhood as an exclusively female status
- Article 3: Reaffirming the rights of women and girls to physical and reproductive integrity
- Article 4: Reaffirming women's rights to freedom of opinion and freedom of expression
- Article 5: Reaffirming women's right to freedom of peaceful assembly and association
- Article 6: Reaffirming women's rights to political participation on the basis of sex
- Article 7: Reaffirming women's rights to the same opportunities as men to participate actively in sports and physical education
- Article 8: Reaffirming the need for the elimination of violence against women
- Article 9: Reaffirming the need for the protection of the rights of the child[100]

It is clear that younger feminists today are as committed as previous generations of radical feminists to searching for root

---

100 <https://www.womensdeclaration.com/en/declaration-womens-sex-based-rights-full-text/>.

causes of problems affecting women in an effort to reveal the truth, and then to fighting the good fight until justice is achieved.

This one thing is certain: Feminists in the tradition of Second Wave feminism will not stand by while patriarchy destroys democracy. We, together with our allies, will continue to hold patriarchy accountable and demand structural change – for the benefit of all.

Bibliography

Ainsworth, Kate. 5 June 2023. 'What Is the PwC Tax Scandal? Who Is Peter-John Collins? Who Knew about It? Why Does It Matter?' *ABC News*. <https://www.abc.net.au/news/2023-06-05/pwc-pricewaterhousecoopers-government-tax-leak-scandal-explained/102409528>.

Akhter, Farida. 1989. 'On the Question of the Reproductive Right: A Personal Reflection'. *Declaration of Comilla*. Dhaka: FINRRAGE/UBINIG Proceedings, pp. 8–11. <http://www.finrrage.org>.

——— 1992. *Depopulating Bangladesh: Essays on the Politics of Fertility*. Dhaka: Narigrantha Prabartana.

Akhter, Farida, Wilma Van Berkel and Natasha Ahmen (Eds). 1989. *Declaration of Comilla*. Dhaka: FINRRAGE/UBINIG Proceedings. <http://www.finrrage.org>.

Allam, Lorena, Calla Wahlquist, Nick Evershed and Miles Herbert. 9 April 2021. 'The 474 Deaths Inside: Tragic Toll of Indigenous Deaths in Custody Revealed'. *The Guardian Australia*. <https://www.theguardian.com/australia-news/2021/apr/09/the-474-deaths-inside-rising-number-of-indigenous-deaths-in-custody-revealed>.

Aly, Waleed. November 2020. 'How Liberalism's Blindspot Let Cancel Culture Bloom'. *The Monthly*.

Aly, Waleed and Scott Stephens. 2022. 'Uncivil Wars: How Contempt Is Corroding Democracy'. *Quarterly Essay*, Issue 87.

Annan, Kofi. 14 September 2017. 'The Crisis of Democracy'. <https://www.kofiannanfoundation.org/supporting-democracy-and-elections-with-integrity/athens-democracy-forum/>.

Antrobus, Blake. 7 December 2021. '"Indescribable Horror": Inquest Told of Hannah Clarke's Final Words, Heroic Last Act Before Death'. News.com.au. <https://www.news.com.au/national/queensland/courts-law/indescribable-horror-coroner-to-probe-shocking-murder-of-hannah-clarke-and-three-kids/news-story/d41b006d6d1861a665cb8abccd4c32e>.

Arditti, Rita, Renate Duelli Klein and Shelley Minden (Eds). 1984/1989/2025. *Test-tube Women: What Future for Motherhood?* London: Pandora Press; Sydney: Allen & Unwin; London: Routledge.

Arendt, Hannah. 25 February 1967. 'Truth and Politics'. *The New Yorker.* <https://www.newyorker.com/magazine/1967/02/25/truth-and-politics>.

——— 1972. *Crises of the Republic: Lying in Politics, Civil Disobedience, On Violence, Thoughts on Politics and Revolution.* New York: Harcourt Brace Janovic.

Armstrong, Louise. 1978. *Kiss Daddy Goodnight: A Speak-Out on Incest.* New York: Pocket Books, Simon and Schuster.

——— 1994. *Rocking the Cradle of Sexual Politics: What Happened When Women Said Incest.* Reading, Massachusetts: Addison-Wesley.

Australian Bureau of Statistics. 5 July 2018. 'Corrective Services Family and Domestic Violence Data Project: Discussion of Findings'. <https://www.abs.gov.au/statistics/people/crime-and-justice/corrective-services-family-and-domestic-violence-data-project-discussion-findings/latest-release>.

Australian Democracy Network. February 2022. 'Confronting State Capture'. <https://australiandemocracy.org.au/statecapture>.

Australian Human Rights Commission. 30 November 2021. 'Set the Standard: Report on the Independent Review into Commonwealth Parliamentary Workplaces (2021)'. <https://humanrights.gov.au/set-standard-2021>.

Australia's National Research Organisation for Women's Safety. November 2020. 'Accurately Identifying the "Person Most in Need of Protection" in Domestic and Family Violence Law'. *Research to Policy and Practice.* Issue 23. <https://www.anrows.org.au/publication/accurately-identifying-the-person-most-in-need-of-protection-in-domestic-and-family-violence-law/>.

Barry, Kathleen. 1979. *Female Sexual Slavery: Understanding the International Dimensions of Women's Oppression.* New York: New York University Press.

——— 1995. *The Prostitution of Sexuality: The Global Exploitation of Women.* London: New York University Press.

——— 2010. *Unmaking War, Remaking Men: How Empathy Can Reshape Our Politics, Our Soldiers and Ourselves.* North Melbourne: Spinifex Press.

——— 2012. 'Abolishing Prostitution: A Feminist Human Rights Treaty'. <https://womensmediacenter.com/news-features/abolishing-prostitution-a-feminist-human-rights-treaty>.

Batty, Rosie with Bryce Corbett. 2016. *A Mother's Story.* Sydney: HarperCollins Publishers.

Bell, Diane and Renate Klein (Eds). 1996. *Radically Speaking: Feminism Reclaimed.* North Melbourne: Spinifex Press.

BIBLIOGRAPHY

Bilek, Jennifer. 26 August 2021. 'Capturing the American Psychological Association: The Engineering of Human Sexual Evolution'. *The 11th Hour Blog*. <https://www.the11thhourblog.com/>.

——— 15 June 2022. 'The Billionaire Family Pushing Synthetic Sex Identities (SSI)'. *Tablet*. <https://www.tabletmag.com/sections/news/articles/billionaire-family-pushing-synthetic-sex-identities-ssi-pritzkers>.

——— 2024. *Transsexual Transgender Transhuman: Dispatches from the 11th Hour*. Mission Beach: Spinifex Press.

Bindel, Julie. 6 July 2015. 'The No Platforming of Radical Feminists'. Talk given at the Quaker Meeting House in Sheffield. Edited transcript at *Feminist Current*. <https://www.feministcurrent.com/2015/06/10/the-no-platforming-of-radical-feminists-a-talk-by-julie-bindel/>.

——— 2017. *The Pimping of Prostitution: Abolishing the Sex Work Myth*. Mission Beach: Spinifex Press.

Bowden, Mark and Matthew Teague. 2022. *The Steal: The Attempt to Overturn the 2020 Election and the People who Stopped It*. New York: Grove Atlantic.

Brodribb, Somer. 1992. *Nothing Mat(t)ers: A Feminist Critique of Postmodernism*. North Melbourne: Spinifex Press.

Brownmiller, Susan. 1975. *Against Our Will: Men, Women and Rape*. London: Secker and Warburg.

Brunskell-Evans, Heather. 2018. 'The Ministry of Trans Truth'. *Spiked*. <https://www.spiked-online.com/2018/12/05/the-ministry-of-trans-truth/>.

——— 2020. *Transgender Body Politics*. Mission Beach: Spinifex Press.

Cabato, Regine. 13 November 2023. 'Philippine Opposition Leader and Duterte Critic Freed After Almost 7 Years'. *The Washington Post*.

Campbell, Andy and Christopher Mathias. 12 August 2017. 'White Supremacist Rally Triggers Violence in Charlottesville'. *Huffington Post*. <https://www.huffpost.com/entry/white-nationalist-charlottesville-virginia_n_598e3fa8e4b0909642972007>.

CBC News. 27 April 2017. '"Democracy As We Know It Is Dead": Filipino Journalists Fight Fake News'. <https://www.cbc.ca/news/world/democracy-as-we-know-it-is-dead-filipino-journalists-fight-fake-news-1.4086920>.

Chesler, Phyllis. 1972. *Women and Madness*. New York: Avon Books.

Chomsky, Noam and Marv Waterstone. 2021. *Consequences of Capitalism*. London: Hamish Hamilton.

Coalition Against Trafficking in Women. <catwinternational.org>.

Contos, Chanel. 28 December 2021. 'Australia Has Been Forced to Face the Truth about the Gender-based Violence behind its "Safe and Happy" Façade'. *The Guardian*. <https://www.theguardian.com/commentisfree/2021/dec/23/australia-has-been-forced-to-face-the-truth-about-the-gender-based-violence-behind-its-safe-and-happy-façade>.

——— 2023. *Consent Laid Bare: Sex, Entitlement & the Distortion of Desire*. Sydney: Pan Macmillan Australia.

Corea, Gena. 1985. *The Mother Machine: Reproductive Technologies from Artificial Insemination to Artificial Wombs*. New York: Harper and Row.

Crenshaw, Kimberlé. 8 June 2017. 'Kimberlé Crenshaw on Intersectionality, More Than Two Decades Later'. Columbia Law School. <https://www.law.columbia.edu/news/archive/kimberle-crenshaw-intersectionality-more-two-decades-later>.

Daly, Mary. 1973. *Beyond God the Father: Toward a Philosophy of Women's Liberation*. Boston: Beacon Press.

de Beauvoir, Simone. 1953. *The Second Sex*. Harmondsworth, Middlesex: Penguin.

Dines, Gail. 2010. *Pornland: How Porn Has Hijacked Our Sexuality*. North Melbourne: Spinifex Press.

Doherty, Ben and Eden Gillespie. 25 June 2023. 'Last Refugee on Nauru Evacuated as Australian Government says Offshore Processing Policy Remains'. *The Guardian*. <https://www.theguardian.com/australia-news/2023/jun/25/last-refugee-on-nauru-evacuated-as-australian-government-says-offshore-processing-policy-remains>.

Donegan, Moira. 21 January 2022. 'Republican Voter Suppression Is Rampant. Manchin and Sinema Are Complicit Now'. *The Guardian*. <https://www.theguardian.com/commentisfree/2022/jan/20/republican-voter-suppression-is-rampant-manchin-and-sinema-are-complicit-now?CMP=Share_iOSApp_Other>.

Donoghoe, Manann, Andre M. Perry, Samantha Gross, Ede Ijjasz-Vasquez, Joseph B. Keller, John W. McArthur, Sanjay Patnaik, Barry G. Rabe, Sophie Roehse, Kemal Kirişci, Landry Signé and David G. Victor. 14 December 2023. 'The Successes and Failures of COP28'. Brookings. <https://www.brookings.edu/articles/the-successes-and-failures-of-cop28/>.

Doran, Matthew. 24 March 2021. 'Prime Minister Scott Morrison Apologises to NewsCorp and Person whose Incident He Exposed'. *ABC News*. <https://www.abc.net.au/news/2021-03-24/pm-scott-morrison-apologises-for-allegation/100024874>.

Duluth Model. <https://www.theduluthmodel.org>.

Dworkin, Andrea. 1979/1981. *Pornography: Men Possessing Women*. New York: Pedigree Books; London: The Women's Press.

BIBLIOGRAPHY

——— 1997. 'Prostitution and Male Supremacy'. In *Life and Death*. New York: Free Press, pp. 139–151.

——— 2004. 'Pornography, Prostitution, and a Beautiful and Tragic Recent History'. In Christine Stark and Rebecca Whisnant (Eds). *Not for Sale: Feminists Resisting Prostitution and Pornography*. North Melbourne: Spinifex Press, pp. 137–45.

Easteal, Patricia. 1994. *Voices of the Survivors*. North Melbourne: Spinifex Press.

Ekman, Kajsa Ekis. 2023. *On the Meaning of Sex: Thoughts about the New Definition of Woman*. Mission Beach: Spinifex Press.

Elton, James. 31 May 2023. 'Treasurer Jim Chalmers Says Naming of PwC partners Placed on Leave Will Happen "In Time"'. *ABC News*. <https://www.abc.net.au/news/2023-05-31/jim-chalmers-pwc-members-to-be-named-publicly/102417308>.

European Centre for Populism Studies. n.d. 'Populism'. <https://www.populismstudies.org/Vocabulary/populism>.

Everyday Sexism Project. <https://www.everydaysexism.com>.

Fabros, Corazon Valdez. 2021. 'From Onlooker to Organizer'. In Renate Klein and Susan Hawthorne (Eds). *Not Dead Yet: Feminism, Passion and Women's Liberation*. Mission Beach: Spinifex Press, pp. 99–106.

Fallon, Claire. 15 August 2017. 'What Is "Whataboutism", And Why Is It Suddenly Everywhere?'. *Huffington Post*. <https://www.huffpost.com/entry/what-is-whataboutism_n_59932909e4b00914164043a4>.

Farley, Melissa. 2003. 'Prostitution and the Invisibility of Harm'. *Women and Therapy*. 26 (3/4), pp. 247–280.

——— 2018a. '#METOO Must Include Prostitution'. *Dignity: A Journal of Sexual Exploitation and Violence*. Vol. 3, No. 1, Article 9.

——— 2018b. 'Risks of Prostitution: When the Person Is the Product'. *Journal of the Association for Consumer Research*. Vol. 3, No. 1, pp. 97–108.

Feminist International Network of Resistance to Reproductive and Genetic Engineering (FINRRAGE). <http://www.finrrage.org>.

Firestone, Shulamith. 1970. *The Dialect of Sex: The Case for Feminist Revolution*. New York: William Morrow.

Fraser, Nancy. 14 October 2013. 'How Feminism Became Capitalism's Handmaiden – and How to Reclaim It'. *The Guardian*. <https://www.theguardian.com/commentisfree/2013/oct/14/feminist-capitalist-handmaiden-neoliberal?CMP=Share_iOSApp_Other>.

——— 2022. *Cannibal Capitalism: How Our System is Devouring Democracy, Care, and the Planet – and What We Can Do about it*. New York: Verso Books.

Fray, Peter and Eric Beecher. 25 May 2021. '"Without Truth, No Democracy Can Stand": Why We Are Calling Out the Prime Minister'. *Crikey*. <https://www.crikey.com.au/2021/05/25/why-are-we-doing-this-scott-morrison/>.

Friedan, Betty. 1963. *The Feminine Mystique*. New York: W.W. Norton.

Funnell, Nina. 22 August 2019. '#LetHerSpeak: Monster Hiding in Plain Sight – Grace Tame's Sexual Abuse Ordeal Revealed'. *News.com.au*. <https://www.news.com.au/lifestyle/real-life/monster-hiding-in-plain-sight-grace-tames-repulsive-schoolgirl-sexual-abuse-ordeal-revealed/news-story/12de77bdf1a2170975b0ef102dd3c59e>.

Gagnon, Jean-Paul. 2018. '2,234 Descriptions of Democracy: An Update to Democracy's Ontological Pluralism'. *Democratic Theory*, 5(1), pp. 92–113. <https://doi.org/10.3167/dt.2018.050107>.

Gaze, Beth. 1994. 'Theories of Free Speech, Pornography and Sexual Equality'. In Tom Campbell and Wojciech Sadurski (Eds). *Freedom of Communication*. Aldershot: Dartmouth.

GCT Team. 2 March 2021. 'Viral Petition by Chanel Contos: 4000+ People Come Forward with Allegations of Sexual Assault'. *Greek City Times*. <https://greekcitytimes.com/2021/03/02/petition-contos-sexual-assault/>.

Goldberg, Jeffrey. 16 November 2020. 'Why Obama Fears for Our Democracy'. *The Atlantic*. <https://www.theatlantic.com/ideas/archive/2020/11/why-obama-fears-for-our-democracy/617087/>.

Greer, Germaine. 1971. *The Female Eunuch*. London: Paladin. First published in Great Britain by MacGibbon and Kee Ltd. 1970.

——— 1999. *The Whole Woman*. London: Doubleday.

Hamilton, Clive. 15 February 2017. 'That Lump of Coal'. *The Conversation*. <https://theconversation.com/that-lump-of-coal-73046>.

Hamilton, Lucy. 30 January 2022. 'Lies, Lies, Lies – and the Lying Liars Who Tell Them'. *The Australian Independent Media Network*. <https://theaimn.com/lies-lies-lies-and-the-lying-liars-who-tell-them/>.

Hanmer, Jalna and Catherine Itzin (Eds). 2001. *Home Truths about Domestic Violence: Feminist Influences on Policy and Practice. A Reader*. Oxford UK: Routledge.

Harrington, Mary, Nimco Ali, Nina Power and Kathleen Stock. 17 December 2021. 'Beyond the Failures of Liberal Feminism'. *Respublica*. <https://www.respublica.org.uk/event/beyond-the-failures-of-liberal-feminism/>.

Hattingh, Michelle. 2017. *I'm the Girl Who Was Raped*. Mission Beach: Spinifex Press.

Hawthorne, Susan. 2004. 'The Political Uses of Obscurantism: Gender Mainstreaming and Intersectionality'. *Development Bulletin*, No. 64, pp. 87

——— 2002/2022. *Wild Politics: Feminism, Globalisation and Bio/diversity*. North Melbourne/Mission Beach: Spinifex Press.

——— 2020. *Vortex: The Crisis of Patriarchy*. Mission Beach: Spinifex Press.

Heberlein, Ann. 2021. *On Love and Tyranny: The Life and Politics of Hannah Arendt*. London: Pushkin Press.

Herman, Judith Lewis. 1981. *Father-Daughter Incest*. Cambridge, Massachusetts: Harvard University Press.

——— 1994. *Trauma and Recovery: From Domestic Abuse to Political Terror*. London: Pandora.

Hett, Benjamin Carter. 2018. *The Death of Democracy: Hitler's Rise to Power and the Downfall of the Weimar Republic*. London: William Heinemann.

Hill, Jess. 2019. *See What You Made Me Do: Power, Control and Domestic Abuse*. Carlton, Victoria: Black Inc. Books.

——— 2021. 'The Reckoning: How #MeToo is Changing Australia'. *Quarterly Essay*, Issue 84.

Hill, Samantha Rose. 28 October 2020. 'Hannah Arendt and the Politics of Truth'. <https://www.resilience.org/stories/2020-10-28/hannah-arendt-and-the-politics-of-truth/>.

hooks, bell. 2013. *Writing Beyond Race: Living Theory and Practice*. New York: Routledge.

Hunter, Rose. 2022. *Body Shell Girl: A Memoir*. Mission Beach: Spinifex Press.

Inside Time Reports. 9 July 2021. 'Trans Women Can Go to Women's Jails, Court Rules'. *Inside Time*. <https://insidetime.org/trans-women-can-go-to-womens-jails-court-rules/>.

Itzin, Catherine (Ed.). 1992. *Pornography, Women, Violence and Civil Liberties*. Oxford: Oxford University Press.

Jaggar, Alison M. and Paula Rothenberg Struhl. 1978. *Feminist Frameworks: Alternative Theoretical Accounts of the Relations between Women and Men*. New York: McGraw-Hill.

Jeffreys, Sheila. 1997. *The Idea of Prostitution*. North Melbourne: Spinifex Press.

——— 1982. 'The Sexual Abuse of Children in the Home'. In Scarlet Friedman and Elizabeth Sarah (Eds). *On the Problem of Men*. London: Women's Press.

——— 2004. 'Prostitution as a Harmful Cultural Practice'. In Christine Stark and Rebecca Whisnant (Eds). *Not for Sale: Feminists Resisting Prostitution and Pornography*. North Melbourne: Spinifex Press, pp. 386–99.

——— 2009. *The Industrial Vagina: The Political Economy of the Global Sex Trade*. Abingdon and New York: Routledge.

——— 2014. *Gender Hurts: A Feminist Analysis of the Politics of Transgenderism*, London: Routledge.

——— 2020. *Trigger Warning: My Lesbian Feminist Life*. Mission Beach: Spinifex Press.

——— 2022. *Penile Imperialism: The Male Sex Right and Women's Subordination*. Mission Beach: Spinifex Press.

Jensen, Robert. 2017. *The End of Patriarchy: Radical Feminism for Men*. Mission Beach: Spinifex Press.

Jepsen, Belinda. 8 March 2019. 'Scott Morrison Just Made the Worst International Women's Day Speech in the History of Forever'. *Mamamia*. <https://www.mamamia.com.au/scott-morrison-international-womens-day/>.

Karp, Paul. 4 October 2023. 'Asylum Seekers Sent to Nauru by Australian Government Only Months After Last Detainees Were Removed'. *The Guardian*. <https://www.theguardian.com/australia-news/2023/oct/04/asylum-seekers-sent-to-nauru-by-australian-government-only-months-after-last-detainees-were-removed>.

Keane, Bernard, Georgia Wilkins and David Hardaker. 25 May 2021. 'A Dossier of Lies and Falsehoods: How Scott Morrison Manipulates the Truth'. *Crikey*. <https://www.crikey.com.au/dossier-of-lies-and-falsehoods/>.

——— 20 December 2021. 'Democracy Lost: Count the Ways Australia Is Falling Behind'. <https://www.crikey.com.au/2021/12/20/democracy-lost-australia-under-threat/>.

——— 10 February 2022. 'Omerta Exploded: Unauthorised Leaks by Tame, Higgins Are Breaking Down the Morrison Model of Power Management'. *Crikey*. <https//www.crikey.com.au/2022/02/10/grace-tame-brittany-higgins-scott-morrison-power/>.

Keane, John, Benjamin Moffitt, Cristobal Rovira Kaltwasser, Jan Zielonka, Takashi Inoguchi, Thamy Pogrebinschi, Ulrike Guerot, Wolfgang Merkel and Yu Keping. 2 November 2016. 'Populism and Democracy: Dr Jekyll and Mr Hyde?' *The Conversation*. <https://theconversation.com/populism-and-democracy-dr-jekyll-and-mr-hyde-67421>.

Kelly, Cait. 2021. 'FOI failure: The Tricks Our Pollies and Bureaucrats Use to Keep Australians in the Dark'. *The New Daily*. <https://thenewdaily.com.au/news/politics/australian-politics/2021/04/25/foi-laws-rex-patrick/>.

Kelly, Liz. 1989. *Surviving Sexual Violence*. Cambridge: Polity Press.

King, Madonna. 20 May 2021. 'Boys to Men: The "Epidemic" Infecting Our Nation That's Not Being Taken Seriously'. *In Queensland*. <https://inqld.

com.au/opinion/2021/05/20/boys-to-men-theres-another-epidemic-infecting-our-nation-and-its-not-being-taken-seriously/>.

Klein, Renate. 1989a. 'New Reproductive Technologies: Who Profits? Who Pays the Price?'. In *Declaration of Comilla*, pp. 12–18. <http://www.finrrage.org/wp-content/uploads/2016/03/Comilla_Proceedings_1989.pdf>.

——— 1989b. *The Exploitation of a Desire: Women's Experiences with In Vitro Fertilisation*. Geelong: Deakin University.

——— (Ed.) 1989c. *Infertility: Women Speak Out about Their Experiences of Reproductive Medicine*. London: Pandora Press.

——— 2017. *Surrogacy: A Human Rights Violation*. Mission Beach: Spinifex Press.

Knaus, Christopher. 20 March 2023. 'Delays Plaguing Australia's FOI System Preventing Scrutiny of Government, Rex Patrick Says'. *The Guardian*. <https://www.theguardian.com/australia-news/2023/mar/20/delays-plaguing-australias-foi-system-preventing-scrutiny-of-government-rex-patrick-says>.

Lahl, Jennifer. February 2022. 'Telling the Truth about Surrogacy in the United States'. The Center for Bioethics and Culture Network. <https://cbc-network.org/wp-content/uploads/2022/02/CBC-Lahl_Telling_the_Truth_about_Surrogacy_in_the_United_States.pdf>.

Lahl, Jennifer, Melinda Tankard Reist and Renate Klein (Eds). 2019. *Broken Bonds: Surrogate Mothers Speak Out*. Mission Beach: Spinifex Press.

Langton, Rae. 1994. 'Speech Acts and Unspeakable Acts'. In Tom Campbell and Wojciech Sadurski (Eds). *Freedom of Communication*. Aldershot: Dartmouth.

Laville, Sandra and Bibi van der Zee. 17 November 2022. 'Draft Cop27 Agreement Fails to Call for "Phase-down" of All Fossil Fuels'. *The Guardian*. <https://www.theguardian.com/environment/2022/nov/17/draft-cop27-agreement-fails-to-call-for-phase-down-of-all-fossil-fuels?ref=upstract.com>.

Lawford-Smith, Holly. 2022. *Gender-Critical Feminism*. Oxford: Oxford University Press.

——— 2023. *Sex Matters: Essays in Gender-Critical Philosophy*. Oxford: Oxford University Press.

Leidholdt, Dorchen and Janice G. Raymond (Eds). 1990. *The Sexual Liberals and the Attack on Feminism*. New York: Pergamon Press.

——— 1993. 'Prostitution: A Violation of Women's Human Rights'. *Cardozo Women's Law Journal*. Vol. 1, No. 1, pp. 133–147.

Leila de Lima. <https://leiladelima.ph>.

Longley, Robert. 29 January 2021. 'What is Democracy? Definition and Examples'. *ThoughtCo.* <https://www.thoughtco.com/democracy-definition-and-examples-5084624>.

Longstaff, Simon. 25 May 2021. 'The Truth Is Precious. Let's Not Take It For Granted'. *Crikey.* <https://crikey.com.au/2021/05/25/truth-is-precious/>.

MacKinnon, Catharine A. 1990. 'Liberalism and the Death of Feminism'. In Dorchen Leidholdt and Janice G. Raymond (Eds). *The Sexual Liberals and the Attack on Feminism.* New York: Pergamon Press, pp. 3–13.

——— July-August 1993. 'Turning Rape into Pornography: Postmodern Genocide'. *Ms Magazine,* pp. 24–30.

——— 1994. *Only Words.* London: HarperCollins.

——— 2006. 'Pornography's Empire'. In *Are Women Human? And Other International Dialogues.* Cambridge, Mass: Belknap Press of Harvard University Press, pp. 112–19.

MacKinnon, Catharine and Andrea Dworkin (Eds). 1997. *In Harms Way: The Pornography Civil Rights Hearings.* Cambridge, Massachusetts: Harvard University Press.

Magennis, Molly. 27 July 2022. '"Extremely Disappointing": First Aboriginal Australian to Become Indigenous Minister Ken Wyatt Slams Pauline Hanson'. *7News.com.au.* <https://7news.com.au/politics/pauline-hanson-storms-out-of-senate-during-acknowledgment-of-country-saying-it-perpetuates-racial-division-c-7658837>.

Masson, Jeffrey. 1989. *Against Therapy.* London: William Collins Sons.

McGhee, Ashlynne. 15 July 2015. 'Darcey Freeman Inquest: Doctors Knew Father Who Threw 4yo off Melbourne's West Gate Bridge Was Violent, Court Hears'. *ABC News* <https://www.abc.net.au/news/2015-07-15/doctors-knew-freeman-was-violent-before-bridge-murder/6620082>.

McLellan, Betty. 1999/2006. *Help! I'm Living With a ~~Man~~ Boy.* North Melbourne: Spinifex Press.

——— 2010. *Unspeakable: A Feminist Ethic of Speech.* Townsville: OtherWise Publications.

——— 2017. *Ann Hannah, My (Un)Remarkable Grandmother: A Psychological Biography.* Mission Beach: Spinifex Press.

Meade, Amanda. 2 April 2021. 'AFR Hit Job on Samantha Maiden Backfires Spectacularly'. *The Guardian.* <https://www.theguardian.com/media/2021/apr/02/afr-hit-job-on-samantha-maiden-backfires-spectacularly>.

MeToo Movement. <https://metoomvmt.org>.

Mies, Maria. 1985. 'Why Do We Need All This? A Call Against Genetic Engineering and Reproductive Technology'. *Women's Studies International Forum* Vol. 8, No. 6, pp. 553–560.

BIBLIOGRAPHY

Mill, John Stuart. 1999. *On Liberty*. New York: Bartleby.com (online books). First published 1859. London: Longman, Roberts & Green.

—— 1873. *Autobiography*. <https://www.earlymoderntexts.com/assets/pdfs/mill1873e.pdf>.

Millett, Kate. 1970/1972. *Sexual Politics*. Garden City, New York: Doubleday; London: Abacus, Sphere Books.

Milligan, Louise, Naomi Selvaratnam and Lauren Day. 8 March 2022. 'Women Who Died After Going to Doomadgee Hospital with a Preventable Disease Were "Badly Let Down," Minister Says'. *ABC News*. <https://www.abc.net.au/news/2022-03-08/doomadgee-hospital-health-service-rhd-women-deaths/100887674>.

Morgan, Robin. 1996. 'Light Bulbs, Radishes, and the Politics of the 21st Century'. In Diane Bell and Renate Klein (Eds). *Radically Speaking: Feminism Reclaimed*. North Melbourne: Spinifex Press, pp. 5–8.

Morse, Dana. 30 November 2022. 'Closing the Gap Report Shows Four Targets Going Backwards as Experts Call for Efforts to "Empower Communities"'. *ABC News*. <https://www.abc.net.au/news/2022-11-30/closing-the-gap-report-released/101713892>.

Mumford, James. 2020. *Vexed: Ethics Beyond Political Tribes*. London: Bloomsbury Publishing.

National Park Service. n.d. 'Declaration of Sentiments'. <https://www.nps.gov/wori/learn/historyculture/declaration-of-sentiments.htm>.

Norma, Caroline and Melinda Tankard Reist (Eds). 2016. *Prostitution Narratives: Stories of Survival in the Sex Trade*. Melbourne: Spinifex Press.

Osborne, Bridget. 29 November 2021. 'Peter Osborne Lists Boris Johnson's Lies in New Website'. *The Cheswick Calendar*. <https://chiswickcalendar.co.uk/peter-oborne-lists-boris-johnsons-lies-in-new-website/>.

Osborne, Peter. 2021. *The Assault on Truth: Boris Johnson, Donald Trump and the Emergence of a New Moral Barbarism*. London: Simon and Schuster. <https://www.simonandschuster.co.uk/books/The-Assault-on-Truth/Peter-Osborne/9781398501003>.

Osborne, Peter and James Willcocks. 2024. 'Lies, Falsehoods and Misrepresentations from Boris Johnson to Keir Starmer'. *Political Lies*. <https://political-lies.co.uk/>.

Pabst, Adrian. 2021. *Postliberal Politics: The Coming Era of Renewal*. Cambridge, UK: Polity Press.

Panahi, Rita. 18 July 2022. 'Safety Must Be Top of Agenda for Women'. *Townsville Bulletin*.

Patrick, Aaron. 31 March 2021. 'PM Caught in Crusade of Women Journos'. *Australian Financial Review*.

Pence, Ellen and Michael Paymar. 1993. *Educational Groups for Men Who Batter: The Duluth Model*. New York: Springer Publishing.

Pengelly, Martin. 3 January 2022. 'Capitol Attack: Cheney Says Republicans Must Choose between Trump and Truth'. *The Guardian*. <https://www.theguardian.com/us-news/2022/jan/02/capitol-attack-liz-cheney-republicans-choose-trump-or-truth?CMP=Share_iOSApp_Other>.

Perkins, Miki. 5 March 2021. 'Anjali Sharma Breaking New Ground in Climate Fight'. *The Sydney Morning Herald*. <https://www.smh.com.au/environment/climate-change/anjali-sharma-breaking-new-ground-in-climate-fight-20210304-p577ym.html>.

Petraitis, Vikki. 1995. *The Frankston Murders: The True Story of Serial Killer Paul Denyer*. Seaford: Nivar Press.

——— 2023. *The Frankston Murders Podcast*. <https://casefilepresents.com/the-frankston-murders>.

Philippine Daily Inquirer. 15 May 2021. 'Jokes, Lies, "Bravado"' (Editorial). <https://opinion.inquirer.net/140252/jokes-lies-bravado>.

Phillips, Jane, Deborah Parker and Michael Woods. 20 September 2018. 'We've Had 20 Aged Care Reviews in 20 Years – Will the Royal Commission Be Any Different?' *The Conversation*. <https://theconversation.com/weve-had-20-reviews-in-20-years-will-the-royal-commission-be-any-different-103347>.

Pizzey, Erin. 1974. *Scream Quietly or the Neighbours Will Hear*. London: Penguin.

Priestly, Angela. 8 March 2019. 'We Don't Want to See "Women Rise" on the Basis of Others Doing Worse, Says Scott Morrison'. *Women's Agenda*. <https://womensagenda.com.au/latest/we-dont-want-to-see-women-rise-on-basis-of-others-doing-worse-scott-morrisons-bizarre-iwd-comments/>.

Pringle, Helen. 23 February 2022. '"Over Himself, over His Own Body and Mind, the Individual Is Sovereign": John Stuart Mill, Freedom of Speech, and the Harm Principle'. <https://www.abc.net.au/religion/john-stuart-mill,-freedom-of-speech,-and-the-harm-principle/13767602>.

Prostitution Research. <prostitutionresearch.com>.

Queally, James. 23 February 2023. 'Harvey Weinstein Sentenced to 16 Years in Prison for Los Angeles Rape'. *Los Angeles Times*.

Ranson, Jan. 11 March 2020. 'Harvey Weinstein Is Sentenced to 23 Years in Prison'. *The New York Times*.

Rappler. 22 July 2022. 'Highlights: Rappler+Briefing on the Social Media Landscape in the 2022 Philippine Elections'. *Rappler.com*. <https://www.

rappler.com/nation/elections/highlights-plus-briefing-social-media-landscape-2022-elections/>.

Rathus, Zoe. 2010. 'Social Science or "Lego-Science"? Presumptions, Politics, Parenting and the New Family Law'. *QUT Law Journal*. Vol. 10. No. 2, pp. 164–190. <https://lr.law.qut.edu.au/article/download/17/16/17-1-34-2-10-20151125.pdf>.

Raymond, Janice G. 1979. *The Transsexual Empire*. London: The Women's Press.

——— 1993/1995. *Women as Wombs: Reproductive Technologies and the Battle over Women's Freedom*. San Francisco: Harper Collins; North Melbourne: Spinifex Press.

——— 1994. *The Transsexual Empire: The Making of the She-Male*. New York: Teachers College Press, Columbia University. Athene Series.

——— 2013/2015. *Not a Choice, Not a Job: Exposing the Myths about Prostitution and the Global Sex Trade*. Nebraska: Potomac Books; North Melbourne: Spinifex Press.

——— 15 September 2015. 'Honoring the Comfort Women'. Radical Feminist Conference, London.

——— 2021. *Doublethink: A Feminist Challenge to Transgenderism*. Mission Beach: Spinifex Press.

Ressa, Maria. 2022. *How to Stand up to a Dictator: The Fight for Our Future*. London: W. H. Allen.

Rich, Adrienne. 1979. *On Lies, Secrets, and Silence: Selected Prose 1966–1978*. New York: W.W. Norton & Company.

Robinson, Jennifer and Keina Yoshida. 2022. *How Many More Women? Exposing How the Law Silences Women*. Sydney: Allen & Unwin.

Roper, Caitlin. 2022. *Sex Dolls, Robots and Woman Hating: The Case for Resistance*. Mission Beach: Spinifex Press.

Ross, W. D. 1928. *The Works of Aristotle Translated into English*. Oxford: Clarendon Press, second edition.

Rowland, Robyn. 1992. *Living Laboratories: Women and Reproductive Technologies*. Sydney: Sun Books; North Melbourne: Spinifex Press; Bloomington: Indiana University Press.

Roy, Arundhati. 2003. *War Talk*. Boston: South End Press.

Royal Commission into Aged Care Quality and Safety. 2020. <https://www.health.gov.au/health-topics/aged-care/aged-care-reforms-and-reviews/royal-commission-into-aged-care-quality-and-safety>.

Rush, Florence. 1980. *The Best Kept Secret: Sexual Abuse of Children*. New York: McGraw-Hill.

RT News. 9 July 2016. '#I Am Not Afraid to Say: Thousands of Sexual Violence Victims Share Harrowing Stories on Facebook'. <https://www.rt.com/news/350338-sexual-violence-online-flashmob/>.

Russell, Diana E. H. 1975. *The Politics of Rape*. New York: Stein and Day.

——— 1990. *Rape in Marriage*. Bloomington: Indiana University Press.

——— (Ed.). 1993. *Making Violence Sexy: Feminist Views on Pornography*. New York: Teachers College Press.

Safe Steps. n.d. 'Family and Domestic Violence Statistics in Australia'. <https://www.safesteps.org.au/statistics/#>.

Sandel, Michael. 12 March 2020. 'Overcoming Division with the Politics of Hope'. ABC Radio National *Big Ideas*. <https://www.abc.net.au/radionational/programs/bigideas/overcoming-division-with-the-politics-of-hope/12030496>.

Schmidt, Vivien A. 2020. *Europe's Crisis of Legitimacy: Governing by Rules and Ruling by Numbers in the Eurozone*. Oxford: Oxford University Press.

Scutt, Jocelynne. 1983. *Even in the Best of Homes: Violence in the Family*. London: Pelican Books.

——— (Ed.) 1988/1989. *The Baby Machine: Commercialisation of Motherhood*. Carlton, Victoria: McCulloch Publishing.

Sharma, Anjali. 15 March 2022. 'Losing This Court Case Feels Like We've Lost Our Chance for a Safe Future'. *The Sydney Morning Herald*. <https://www.smh.com.au/environment/climate-change/losing-this-court-case-feels-like-we-ve-lost-our-chance-for-a-safe-future-20220315-p5a4sc.html>.

Shepard, Melanie F. and Ellen Pence. 1999. *Coordinated Community Response to Domestic Violence: Lessons from the Duluth Model*. Thousand Oaks, California: Sage Publications.

Slezak, Michael. 8 August 2016. 'Asylum Seekers: Australia's Silence over "On-water Matters" Faces Legal Test'. *The Guardian*. <https://www.theguardian.com/australia-news/2016/aug/08/asylum-seekers-australias-silence-over-on-water-matters-faces-legal-test>.

Smiley, Cherry. 2023. *Not Sacred, Not Squaws: Indigenous Feminism Redefined*. Mission Beach: Spinifex Press.

Soutphommasane, Tim. 2019. *On Hate*. Melbourne: Melbourne University Press.

Spallone, Patricia and Deborah Lynn Steinberg (Eds). 1987. *Made to Order: TheMyth of Reproductive and Genetic Progress*. Oxford: Pergamon Press, The Athene Series.

Spender, Dale. 1980. *Man Made Language*. London: Routledge and Kegan Paul.

——— 1982. *Women of Ideas (And What Men Have Done to Them): From Aphra Behn to Adrienne Rich*. London: Ark Paperbacks.

Stanford Encyclopedia of Philosophy. n.d. 'Truth'. <https://plato.stanford.edu/entries/truth>.

——— n.d. 'Identity Politics'. <https://plato.stanford.edu/entries/identity-politics/>.

Stark, Christine and Rebecca Whisnant (Eds). 2004. *Not for Sale: Feminists Resisting Prostitution and Pornography*. North Melbourne: Spinifex Press.

Statista Research Department. 4 April 2024. 'Bushfires in Australia – Statistics and Facts'. Statista. <https://www.statista.com/topics/6125/bushfires-in-australia/#topicHeader_wrapper>.

Sullivan, Mary Lucille. 2004. 'Can Prostitution Be Safe? Applying Occupational Health and Safety Codes to Australia's Legalised Brothel Prostitution'. In Christine Stark and Rebecca Whisnant (Eds). *Not for Sale: Feminists Resisting Prostitution and Pornography*. North Melbourne: Spinifex Press.

——— 2007. *Making Sex Work: A Failed Experiment with Legalised Prostitution*. North Melbourne: Spinifex Press.

Summers, Anne. 1975. *Damned Whores and God's Police*. Ringwood, Victoria: Penguin.

Tadros, Edmund. 16 May 2023. 'Senator: Give Me the Names of the 50 PwC Partners in Tax Leak Emails'. *The Australian Financial Review*. <https://www.afr.com/companies/professional-services/senator-give-me-the-names-of-the-50-pwc-partners-in-tax-leak-emails-20230516-p5d8rv>.

Tankard Reist, Melinda and Abigail Bray (Eds). 2011. *Big Porn Inc: Exposing the Harms of the Global Porn Industry*. North Melbourne: Spinifex Press.

Tankard Reist, Melinda (Ed.) 2022. *"He Chose Porn over Me": Women Harmed by Men Who Use Porn*. Mission Beach: Spinifex Press.

Taylor, Jessica. 6 October 2022. 'Award-winning Novelist Chimamanda Ngozi Adichie Who Was Cancelled for Saying "Transwomen Are Transwomen" Insists She Will Continue to "Say What She Thinks" and Is Happy to "Accept the Consequences"'. *Daily Mail*. <https://www.dailymail.co.uk/femail/article-11286775/Chimamanda-Ngozi-Adichie-continue-say-thinks-accused-transphobia.html>.

Thompson, Denise. 1996. 'The Self-Contradiction of Post-Modernist Feminism'. In Diane Bell and Renate Klein (Eds). *Radically Speaking: Feminism Reclaimed*. North Melbourne: Spinifex Press, pp. 325–38.

Tiernan, Anne. 2021. 'Power, Populism and Principles. The Existential Threat to Australian Democracy'. *Griffith Review* 75. <https://www.griffithreview.com/articles/power-populism-and-principles/>.

Times Up Movement. <https://www.abc.net.au/news/2023-01-22/times-up-metoo-group-halts-operations/101880136>.
Truth and Reconciliation Commission. <https://www.justice.gov.za/trc>.
Tyler, Meagan. 8 March 2021. 'Can Feminism Be Saved from Identity Politics?' *ABC Religion & Ethics*. <https://www.abc.net.au/religion/can-feminism-be-saved-from-identity-politics/11646084>.
The Uluru Statement. <https://ulurustatement.org>.
Ward, Elizabeth. 1984. *Father-Daughter Rape*. London: The Women's Press.
The Washington Post. 20 January 2021 (updated). 'In Four Years, President Trump Made 30,573 False or Misleading Claims'. <https://www.washingtonpost.com/graphics/politics/trump-claims-database/>.
West, Andrew. 29 January 2020. 'Human Rights, Neoliberalism and the Morals of the Market'. *The Religion and Ethics Report*. <https://www.abc.net.au/radionational/programs/religionandethicsreport/january-29-2020/11909880>.
––– 8 July 2020. 'Ethics Beyond Political Tribes'. *ABC Radio National*. <https://www.abc.net.au/listen/programs/religionandethicsreport/vexed-ethics-beyond-political-tribes/12434756>.
Whyte, Jessica. 2019. *The Morals of the Market: Human Rights and the Rise of Neoliberalism*. London: Verso.
Williams, Janice. 30 October 2017. 'Harvey Weinstein Accusers. Over 80 Women Now Claim Producer Sexually Assaulted or Harassed Them'. *Newsweek*. <https://www.newsweek.com/harvey-weinstein-accusers-sexual-assault-harassment-696485>.
Women's Declaration International. n.d. 'Declaration on Women's Sex-Based Rights: Full Text'. <https://www.womensdeclaration.com/en/declaration-womens-sex-based-rights-full-text/>.
Wong, Penny. 29 March 2019. 'McKinnon Prize in Political Leadership Oration'. <https://www.pennywong.com.au/media-hub/speeches/mckinnon-prize-in-political-leadership-oration-melbourne-university-29-03-2019/>.
Wright, Clare. 29 January 2021. 'Friday Essay: Masters of the Future or Heirs of the Past? Mining, History and Indigenous Ownership'. *The Conversation*. <https://theconversation.com/friday-essay-masters-of-the-future-or-heirs-of-the-past-mining-history-and-indigenous-ownership-153879>.
Wright, Colin. *Reality's Last Stand*. <https://www.realityslaststand.com/>.

Index

Abbott, Tony, 114, 115
Aboriginal and Torres Strait Islander Voice
　referendum on, 4–5, 102–3, 162
Aboriginal Australians. *See* Indigenous Australians
Age of Enlightenment, 8, 120
AI (artificial intelligence), 166
Akhter, Farida, 27–8
Albanese, Anthony, 4, 69
　and climate action, 95
　and Indigenous Australians, 99
　and Murugappan family, 83
　and PwC scandal, 116
alcohol and drug additions, 93, 105
Ali, Nimco, 122
allies and alliances, 166–8
'alternative facts', 84–5
Aly, Waleed, 126, 144–5
Annan, Kofi, 10
Anning, Fraser, 70
Apartheid, 3–4
Aquinas, St Thomas, 32
Arendt, Hannah, 19–20, 85
Aristotle, 3, 32
Arthur, Sister Marie Brigid, 57
artificial intelligence (AI), 166
Atkinson, Judy, 170
Australian Democracy Network, 68

Banducci, Brad, 132
Bannon, Steve, 89
Barry, Kathleen
　on pornography, 20
　on prostitution, 25
　on war, 35
Bates, Laura, 47
Bell, Diane, 86
Bester, Nicolaas Ockert, 51
Biden, Joe, 72–3
Bien-Aimé, Taina, 25
Bilek, Jennifer, 43
'Biloela family' (Murugappan family), 82–3
Bindel, Julie, 127–8
Black Liberation, 102
Black Lives Matter movement, 111, 112
Blair, Tony, 74
Blum, Léon, 142
Booth, Betty, 99
Bragg, Andrew, 116
Brodribb, Somer, 40
Browne, Bill, 114
Brownmiller, Susan, 170
Brunskell-Evans, Heather, v, 43
Burke, Tarana, 45, 46
Burney, Linda, 5

Cady Stanton, Elizabeth, 17
cancel culture, 125–6, 130–1, 153
　See also censorship
capitalism
　and feminism, 149–50
　and greed, 131–2
　narratives of, 163–4
　and neoliberalism, 79–81
　and patriarchy, 41, 79
　and postliberalism, 122

censorship, 129–30, 165–6
  See also cancel culture
Chalmers, Jim, 116
Cheney, Liz, 65
Chesler, Phyllis, 36–7
childcare, devaluing of, 133
children
  and climate action, 56–7
  custody of, 105–6
  development of, 98–9
  and domestic violence, 29–30, 81–2, 100–1, 104–5, 139
  future of, 159
  and homelessness, 139
  incarceration of, 165
  and pornography, 21–2
  sexual assault and abuse of, 25–6, 45, 93
  theft or removal of, 4, 98–9, 104–6, 161
China
  and whataboutism, 110
  women and girls in, 158
Chomsky, Noam, 79
Christianity, 39, 63, 141
  See also religion
civil liberties, 61
civil rights, 22
  See also human rights
Clarke, Hannah, and family, 81
Clennell, Andrew, 109
climate action, 56–8, 133–4, 165
  allies in, 167
  and gradualism, 94–5
Clinton, Hillary, 144–5
coercive control, 105
Collins, Peter-John, 115
Combahee River Collective, 148
Comilla Declaration, 27
consent, sexual, 50, 170–2
contempt, 142, 144–5, 147
Contos, Chanel, 50, 55, 171–2
Conway, Kellyanne, 84–5
cooperation vs competition, 124, 163–4
Cordingly, Toya, 138
corporate influence, 68, 94
  See also capitalism

Correspondence Theory, 3
Covid-19, 72, 96
Crenshaw, Kimberlé, 154–5
cultural heritage, 134

Daly, Mary, 36
de Beauvoir, Simone, 32
de Lima, Leila, 76–8
Declaration of Independence (USA), 120–1
Declaration of Sentiments (1848), 39
Declaration on Women's Sex Based Rights, 170, 172
defamation, 54–5
democracy
  abuse of, 64–9
  definitions and types of, 5–10, 163
  ideals and principles of, 6, 60–1
  threats to, 62–3
Denyer, Paul, 107–8
Dines, Gail, 170
disability, people with, 81, 82, 84, 154, 159, 162, 165
discrimination, by sex, 32–5
discrimination, religious or ethnic, 140, 145, 158
  See also racism
disinformation, 72–8, 87, 89
  in elections, 125
  and gender, 153
  and Indigenous Voice referendum, 102
  See also lies
divorce and marital separation, 105–6, 158
Dixon, Eurydice, 137
domestic violence. *See under* violence
Donegan, Moira, 66
Duluth Model (against domestic abuse), 30–1
Duterte, Rodrigo, 76–7, 141
Duterte, Sara, 78
Dworkin, Andrea, 170
  on language and naming, 36
  on pornography, 20–2
  on prostitution, 24

INDEX

egalitarianism, 139, 149
  in Australia, 121
Eisen, Anthony, 132
Ekman, Kajsa Ekis, 169
elections
  in Australia, 121
  conduct of, 60–1, 65–6, 72–5
  and democracy, 6, 60–1
  in the Philippines, 77–8, 125
  in USA, 72–3, 144–5
  and women, 18
  See also voting rights
elites, 140, 142, 145–6
environmental harm and activism, 133–4, 165
  See also climate action
equalism, 102–8, 117, 163
  definition of, 91, 103
  See also equality
equality
  disadvantages and limitations of, 102, 108, 163
  before the law, 6
  and liberalism, 8, 157
  and neoliberalism, 80
  and populism, 140
  between races, 71, 102–3
  between the sexes, 9–10, 22, 62, 92, 103
  and transgender activism, 153
  See also equalism; inequality
erasure of women, 19, 32, 37, 41–4, 153
eugenics, 43
Everyday Sexism Project, 47–8
extremism, political, 63, 71–2

Farley, Melissa, 23–4
fascism, 2, 62
Fawcett, Millicent Garrett, 18
Federal Integrity Commission (Australia), 67–8
female genital mutilation (FGM), 152–3
feminism and feminists
  campaigns fought by, 94–5
  definitions and types of, 10–13
  of the future, 157–9
  and individualism, 149–50

liberal/postliberal, 11, 122–3
  radical, 12–13, 157
  Second Wave, 5, 17–19, 168
Feminist International Network of Resistance to Reproductive and Genetic Engineering (FINRRAGE), 27–8
Feminist International Network on the New Reproductive Technologies (FINNRET), 27
'femocrats', 11
Ferry, Jules, 142
Firestone, Shulamith, 33
First Nations Voice. *See* Aboriginal and Torres Strait Islander Voice
Floyd, George, 112
fossil fuels, 94, 133–4
  See also climate action
Fraser, Nancy, 149–50
Fream, Debbie, 107
freedom of information (FOI), 67, 113–14
freedom of speech, 9, 124–31, 143, 163, 165–6
Freeman, Darcey, and family, 81–2
Freud, Sigmund, 26
Friedan, Betty, 33
fundamentalism, 141, 158, 165

Gagnon, Jean-Paul, 5
Gay Liberation, 41, 62, 102, 148, 153
gender
  definition of, 86
  and language, 85–6, 152–3
  and quotas, 92
  See also transgender activism
George, Shakaya, 99
globalisation, 32, 123, 143, 146
Goldberg, Jeffrey, 59
gradualism, 91–101
  and aged care, 96–7
  definition of, 91
  and Indigenous Australians, 97–100
  and women's safety, 100–1
greed, 131–5
Greer, Germaine, 170
  on feminism of the future, 157–8

on hate, 29, 138
on marriage, 33–4
on transgenderism, 127, 169
Guerot, Ulrike, 142–3
guns and other weapons, 92
Guterres, António, 25
Gutierrez, Ambra, 45–6

Hamilton, Clive, 94
Hamilton, Lucy, 75
Hanson, Pauline, 70
Hanson-Young, Sarah, 49
Harrington, Mary, 122
hatred, racial, 21, 70
Hawke, Bob, 100
Hawthorne, Susan
   on feminism of the future, 158–9
   on neoliberalism, 79, 80–1
   on obscurantism, 40–1
   on wild politics, 2
heritage, destruction of, 134
Hester, Veronica, 57
Hett, Benjamin Carter, 62
hideandseekism, 113–17
Higgins, Brittany, 48–9, 53–4, 112
Hill, Jess, 2, 136, 170–1
Hitler, Adolf, 62–3
Hobbes, Thomas, 8, 120
Hockey, Joe, 115
Holt, Harold, 121
hooks, bell, 41, 170
Howard, John, 80, 105
human rights, 61
   and community responsibilities, 61, 72, 80–1, 120
   and neoliberalism, 80, 89
   origins of, 8
   and prostitution, 24–5
   See also civil liberties
humiliation, 13, 142, 146–7
hyper-individualism, 89, 139, 148, 150
   See also individualism

#IAmNotAfraidToSay, 46
identity politics, 148–55, 163
   history and definition of, 148–9
   and transgender activism, 151–5

immigration, 70, 82
   and populism, 140
Indigenous Australians, 4
   acknowledgement of, 70
   and alliances, 167–8
   cultural heritage of, 134
   deaths in custody of, 97–8, 111–12
   and the free market, 82
   and gradualism, 97–100
   violence against, 137
   See also Aboriginal and Torres Strait Islander Voice; racism
individualism
   and capitalism, 149–50
   and feminism, 149–50
   harm caused by, 119
   and liberalism, 79
   and neoliberalism, 150
   See also hyper-individualism
inequality
   economic, 132–3, 140
   and feminism, 149
   and freedom of speech, 131
   and greed, 132
   ingrained, 63, 69–71
   and liberalism, 8
   and power, 52
   structural, 10, 31, 93
   See also equalism; equality
International Peace Bureau, 2
intersectionality, 12, 154–5
41
Iran, women in, 158
Islam, 71, 145, 158
   See also religion
'isms', 91

Jaggar, Alison, 10–13
Jaurès, Jean, 142
Javate-De Dios, Aurora, 25
Jeffreys, Sheila
   on erasure of women, 43
   on the future, 168
   on prostitution, 24
   on transgenderism, 127, 128–9, 169
Jenkins, Kate, 51
Jensen, Robert, 35

INDEX

Job Seeker allowance, 133
Johnson, Boris, 14, 74–5
journalists
   female, 48, 53, 55, 77, 170
   legal action against, 26, 54–5, 77–8
   role of, 52–3, 58
Joyce, Alan, 132
Juukan Gorge, 134

Kant, Immanuel, 8
'Kate', 49, 54
Kaur, Jasmeen, 138
Keane, Bernard, 67, 71–2, 95
Keane, John, 143
Kelly, Liz, 170
King, Madonna, 50
Klein, Renate
   on postmodernism, 86
   on surrogacy, 27–8

Lahl, Jennifer, 28
language
   and erasure of women, 41–4
   gender-neutral, 85–6, 152
   and naming, 36–7
   and obscurantism, 39–41
   and silencing, 37–9
Lawford-Smith, Holly, 129, 169
Lehrmann, Bruce, 53–4
Leidholdt, Dorchen, 25
lesbian groups, 41, 148, 153
Ley, Sussan, 57
LGBTQIA+, 41, 153, 155
liberalism, 87–8
   definition of, 7–10, 87
   and freedom of speech, 124–31
   and greed, 131–5
   history of, 120–1, 123
   and individualism, 78–9, 87–8, 120
   problems with, 121–31, 148–55
   today, 121–4
libertarianism, 8n6, 79, 88–9
   in the USA, 89
lies
   consequences of, 19, 74–6
   and disinformation, 72–7
   and liberalism, 87–8

   and libertarianism, 88–9
   nature of, 20, 85
   and neoliberalism, 81
   and politics, 56, 59–60, 71–8, 117
   prevalence of, 14, 85
   and social media, 125
   and transgender activism, 169–70
   and Voice referendum, 102
   See also disinformation
Locke, John, 8, 120
Longley, Robert, 6
Longstaff, Simon, 76

Maasarwe, Aiia, 138
MacKinnon, Catharine, 21–2, 170
Magna Carta, 8
Maiden, Samantha, 48, 53
Major, John, 74
Make America Great Again (MAGA) movement, 89, 140
   See also Trump, Donald
Mandela, Nelson, 3–4
March4Justice, 51, 55, 112
Marcos, Ferdinand Jr, 77, 125
marriage
   and gender roles, 33–4
   and racial difference, 103
   rape in, 11, 93
   as a trap, 34
masculinity
   and postmodernism/post-structuralism, 40
   and war, 35
Meade, Amanda, 53
Meagher, Jill, 137
Melnichenko, Anastasia, 46
men's rights groups, 104, 105
meritocracy, 92, 146–7
#MeToo movement, 45–7, 55, 111, 136, 170
Milano, Alyssa, 46
Mill, Harriet Taylor, 9–10
Mill, John Stuart, 9–10
Miller, Michael, 110
Millett, Kate, 34
Milligan, Louise, 54
Molnar, Nick, 132

Morgan, Robin, 13
Morrison, Scott
  and allegations by 'Kate', 49
  and climate action, 94–5
  and democracy, 66–9
  and gender, 92
  and gradualism, 95–7
  and immigration, 114
  and Indigenous Voice referendum, 4
  and lies, 14, 75
  and March4Justice, 51
  and Murugappan family, 83
  and sexual assault in Parliament House, 109–10
motherhood, 172
  and language, 152
  surrogate, 28 (*See also* surrogacy)
  and transgender activism, 85, 152
Mott, Lucretia, 17
Muller, Denis, 113
Mumford, James, 64
Murphy, Meghan
  on erasure of women, 43
  on transgenderism, 127, 130
Murugappan family, 82–3

narratives
  changing of, 159, 162
  false, 164
  importance of, 162–4, 166
  and nationalism, 162–3
national security, 114
nationalism, 162–3
  See also populism
neoliberalism, 79–84
  in Australia, 79–80
  definition of, 79
  history of, 123–4
  and human rights, 80
  and individualism, 122–4
  and money, 131–2
  and populism, 146
News Corp, 109–10
Ngozie, Chimamanda Adichie, 130

Obama, Barack, 59–60
obscurantism, 39–41, 84

O'Neill, Deborah, 116
'on-water matters', 114–15
Osborne, Peter, 74–5

Pabst, Adrian, 122, 132
Page, Katie, 132
Pankhurst, Emmeline, 18
Parliament of Australia
  disrespect for, 67–8, 143
  history of, 121
  and Indigenous Australians, 70
    (*See also* Aboriginal and Torres Strait Islander Voice)
  sexual assault and harassment in, 48–54, 109–10, 112
  women in, 92
  See also elections; politicians; voting rights
Patrick, Aaron, 53
Patrick, Rex, 113–14
Paymar, Michael, 31
Payne, Marise, 51
Pence, Ellen, 30–1, 170
Pence, Mike, 73
Petraitis, Vikki, 108
Philippines
  democracy in, 76–8, 125
  and populism, 141
Pinikura people, 134
Pizzey, Erin, 29–30
Pocock, Barbara, 116
politicians
  duty of, 60
  independent, 55–6, 167
  and lies, 72–4, 85
  and tribalism, 64–9
  See also Parliament of Australia
politics, wild, 2
populism
  causes of, 141–7
  and contempt, 144–5
  definition of, 140
  and Donald Trump, 141
  and humiliation, 146–7
  and powerlessness, 142–3
  and social media, 144
pornography, 12, 20–2

and greed, 134–5
harm caused by, 22
history and definition of, 21
purpose of, 20–2
and violence, 135–7
Porter, Christian, 49, 54
postliberalism, 122–3
postmodernism/poststructuralism, 40–1, 78, 84–7
poverty, 9–10, 69–70, 132, 158
and neoliberalism, 81
and populism, 143
See also inequality: economic; salaries and wages
Power and Control Wheel (of domestic violence), 31
power imbalances, 19, 132–3, 160–1
Power, Nina, 122
PricewaterhouseCoopers (PwC), 115–16
Priestly, Angela, 92
Princi, Ava, 57
Pringle, Helen, 9
prisons
and asylum seekers, 162
and transgenderism, 106–7, 154
and women, 165
prostitution, 12, 23–4
definition of, 23, 25
and greed, 134–5
harms caused by, 24–5
as 'sex work', 23
in Thailand, 158
and violence, 135–7
psychiatry, 36–7
public service, resourcing of, 115
Puutu Kunti Kurrama people, 134

racism, 69–70, 154–5
in Australia, 87, 121
in health care, 99–100
and language, 87
and neoliberalism, 82
and populism, 140
and quotas, 92
and violence, 137
See also Indigenous Australians

rape
and the legal system, 26, 136–7
in marriage, 11
See also violence
Rathus, Zoe, 106
Raymond, Janice G., 25, 169
on censorship, 129
on erasure of women, 43
on transgenderism, 42–3, 127, 129
Reagan, Ronald, 79
refugees and asylum-seekers, 82–3, 114–15, 162
and populism, 140
refuges for women, 11, 100
religion, 6, 8, 140, 165
See also Christianity; Islam
Ressa, Maria, v, 2, 77–8, 125
Rich, Adrienne, 37–8
Rio Tinto, 134
Robinson, Jennifer, 26, 54–5, 171
Roper, Caitlin, 136
Rose Hill, Samantha, 19
Rousseau, Jean-Jacques, 8
Rowling, J. K., 127
Roy, Arundhati, 2
royal commissions, 95–101
Rukeyser, Muriel, v
Russell, Natalie, 107

salaries and wages, 69, 80, 97, 98, 132–3
See also inequality: economic
Sandel, Michael, 121–2, 146–7
Sandy, Adele, 99
Santos, Ray Jr, 78
Saunders, Luca Gwyther, 57
School Strike for Climate movement, 57
science
and libertarianism, 88
and populism, 63–4, 73, 140
and postmodernism, 84
and transgender activism, 131–2
Scutt, Jocelynne, 30
secrecy, 68, 113–16
Seneca Falls Convention (1848), 17, 39
Sessions, Jeff, 109
sex and gender, definitions of, 86

sex discrimination
  harm caused by, 34–5
  history of, 32–3
  and language, 36–41
'sex work', 23
  See also prostitution
sex-based crimes, 170–2
  See also rape; violence
sexual assault, 25–6
  and the law, 26, 53–5
  See also rape; violence
sexual harassment, 11, 46–8
  impunity for, 112, 171
  and journalists, 55
  laws against, 93–4
  in Parliament House, 52, 109–10
  prevalence of, 137
  in prisons, 107
  See also #MeToo movement
Sharma, Anjali, 56–7
Shepard, Melanie F., 31
Shorten, Bill, 85–6
Sikulu, Joseph, 133
slavery, 21, 37, 92
social media, 166
  and bullying/harassment, 125–6
  and censorship, 129–30
  and elections, 125–6
  and freedom of expression, 124–5
  and lies, 77
  and populism, 140, 144
  and tribalism, 63–4, 125
socialism
  and feminism, 10–11, 34
  and John Stuart Mill/Harriet Mill, 37
  and patriarchy, 34
South Africa, 3–4
Soutphommasane, Tim, 70
sovereign citizen phenomenon, 88–9
sovereignty of the individual, 9–10
Spender, Dale, 38, 39–40
Spinoza, Benedict de, 120
sport, and transgender activism, 108, 154, 172
state capture, 68, 143
Stephens, Scott, 144–5
stereotyping, sexual, 32–3

Stevens, Elizabeth, 107
Stock, Kathleen, 122, 127
Struhl, Paula Rothenberg, 10–13
Stutchbury, Michael, 53
Suffragettes/Suffragists, 18
Summers, Anne, 34
surrogacy, 12, 20, 27–8, 31, 160, 165

Tame, Grace, 50–1
Tankard Reist, Melinda, 28, 135–6
Teach Us Consent campaign, 171
terra nullius, 4
Thailand, women in, 158
Thatcher, Margaret, 79
Thompson, Denise, 40
Thunberg, Greta, 56
Tiernan, Anne, 67–8
TIME'S UP, 46–7
trafficking of women for sex.
  See prostitution
'trans exclusionary radical feminists' (TERFs), 12, 127
transgender activism, 12, 106–7
  and cancel culture, 126–9, 153
  and free speech, 165–6
  and identity politics, 151–5
  and language, 85–6, 127, 152–3, 169–70
transgender people, 42–3
  and prisons, 106–7, 154
  and safety, 153–4
  and sport, 108, 154
transparency, 4, 113–14, 116, 167
tribalism, 1, 60, 147
  and politicians, 63–9
  and social media, 124–5
Trump, Donald, 14
  and 'alternative facts', 84–5
  and elections, 65–6, 72–4
  and extremism, 71
  and libertarianism, 89
  and populism, 140–1
  and tribalism, 63
  and white supremacists, 109
truth
  definition of, 3–5
  rational vs factional, 20

INDEX

as relative, 73–4
Truth and Reconciliation Commission (South Africa), 4
Turnbull, Malcolm, 4, 114
Tutu, Desmond, 4
Tyler, Meagan, 122, 150
tyrants and tyranny, 2, 17, 62–3

Uluru Statement from the Heart, 4–5
  See also Aboriginal and Torres Strait Islander Voice to Parliament
unemployment, 24, 69, 132–3, 168
Unite the Right rally (2017), 71, 109

Valdez Fabros, Corazon, 2
Villanova College (Brisbane), 50
violence
  accountability for, 136–7, 171
  activism against, 165, 170–2
  and children, 139
  domestic, 28–32, 138–9
  and equalism, 104–8
  government responses to, 100–1, 112
  and language, 86–7
  by men, 2, 11, 12–13, 81–2, 86–7
  against other men, 137
  police responses to, 104–5
  and racism, 137
  rates of, 165
  sexual, 135–7, 138–9, 170–1
  on the street, 137–8
  and transgender activism, 106–8
  by women, 104, 111
  See also #MeToo movement

voting rights, 18
  for African-Americans, 121
  in Australia, 121
  for Indigenous Australians, 97, 121
  for women, 121
  See also elections
Vukotic, Masa, 137

waititoutism, 111–12
war
  Australia's actions in, 162–3
  and masculinity, 35
  a world without, 2
Waterstone, Marv, 79
Weinstein, Harvey, 45–6
whataboutism, 108–11
White Australia Policy, 121
white supremacists, 41, 63, 70, 71–2, 109, 141
Whitlam, Gough, 121
Whyte, Jessica, 80
Wikramanayake, Shemara, 132
Women's Aid (UK), 29
Women's Declaration International (WDI), 17n11, 172
Women's Liberation Movement, 102, 123, 165
Wong, Penny, 49, 70–1
Wright, Clare, 134
Wright, Colin, 131n83

Yoshida, Keina, 26, 54–5, 171

Zhao Lijian, 110

Other books by Betty McLellan available from Spinifex Press

Beyond Psychoppression:
A Feminist Alternative Therapy

A guide to therapy, *Beyond Psychoppression* explores the intersection between the personal and the political. Betty McLellan surveys the development of psychotherapy and exposes the oppressive techniques of Freudian psychoanalysis, humanistic therapies, lesbian sex therapy, and new age and popular therapies. She challenges the myths about women's mental and emotional illness.

ISBN 9781875559336   eBook available

Help! I'm Living with a ~~Man~~ Boy

This book comprises forty-one scenarios many women will be all too familiar with, like finding towels on the bathroom floor. How do you go about making men understand the difference between helping out with the housework and actually doing it? And what about violence? *Help! I'm Living with a ~~Man~~ Boy* provides suggestions and advice for dealing with these common situations.

Boys will be boys – and that, at least in the eyes of women, is the real trouble … With a mixture of sensitivity and humour McLellan puts forward some thoughtful strategies to help men understand the difference between mumbled promises of future help and solid action.
—Peter Laud, *Sunday Times*

ISBN 9781876756628   eBook available

Ann Hannah, My (Un)Remarkable Grandmother:
A Psychological Biography

This astute psychological biography tells the story of Ann Hannah, Betty's grandmother, who was an ordinary, no-nonsense, practical working-class woman. Using Ann Hannah's everyday expressions as clues, the author delves further to uncover the truths about her life. Written with a sharp feminist consciousness that displays both compassion and intellect, it provides valuable insight into the lives of many (un)remarkable women whose lives may have gone unnoticed by historians but whose experiences shed so much light on the realities faced by women throughout the 1900s.

ISBN 9781925581287   eBook available

*If you would like to know more about
Spinifex Press, write to us for a free catalogue, visit our
website or email us for further information
on how to subscribe to our monthly newsletter.*

Spinifex Press
PO Box 105
Mission Beach QLD 4852
Australia

www.spinifexpress.com.au
women@spinifexpress.com.au